MznLnx

Missing Links Exam Preps

Exam Prep for

Comparative Economic Systems

Schnitzer, 8th Edition

The MznLnx Exam Prep is your link from the texbook and lecture to your exams.
The MznLnx Exam Preps are unauthorized and comprehensive reviews of your textbooks.

All material provided by MznLnx and Rico Publications (c) 2010
Textbook publishers and textbook authors do not particpate in or contribute to these reviews.

MznLnx

Rico
Publications

Exam Prep for Comparative Economic Systems
8th Edition
Schnitzer

Publisher: Raymond Houge
Assistant Editor: Michael Rouger
Text and Cover Designer: Lisa Buckner
Marketing Manager: Sara Swagger
Project Manager, Editorial Production: Jerry Emerson
Art Director: Vernon Lowerui

Product Manager: Dave Mason
Editorial Asitant: Rachel Guzmanji
Pedagogy: Debra Long
Cover Image: Jim Reed/Getty Images
Text and Cover Printer: City Printing, Inc.
Compositor: Media Mix, Inc.

(c) 2010 Rico Publications
ALL RIGHTS RESERVED. No part of this work covered by the copyright may be reproduced or used in any form or by an means--graphic, electronic, or mechanical, including photocopying, recording, taping, Web distribution, information storage, and retrieval systems, or in any other manner--without the written permission of the publisher.

Printed in the United States
ISBN:

For more information about our products, contact us at:
Dave.Mason@RicoPublications.com

For permission to use material from this text or product, submit a request online to:
Dave.Mason@RicoPublications.com

Contents

CHAPTER 1
The American Century — 1

CHAPTER 2
Capitalism as an Economic System — 11

CHAPTER 3
The United States — 21

CHAPTER 4
Japan — 34

CHAPTER 5
Germany — 42

CHAPTER 6
Socialism as an Economic System — 48

CHAPTER 7
The Rise and Fall of Communism — 61

CHAPTER 8
The Russian Federation — 68

CHAPTER 9
Poland, the Czech Republic, and Hungary — 76

CHAPTER 10
Problems of the Less Developed Countries — 79

CHAPTER 11
China — 84

CHAPTER 12
India — 89

CHAPTER 13
Latin America: Argentina, Brazil, and Mexico — 93

CHAPTER 14
Africa: Nigeria and South Africa — 100

CHAPTER 15
World Economic Integration — 106

CHAPTER 16
The Twenty-First Century — 116

ANSWER KEY — 123

TO THE STUDENT

COMPREHENSIVE

The *MznLnx* Exam Prep series is designed to help you pass your exams. Editors at MznLnx review your textbooks and then prepare these practice exams to help you master the textbook material. Unlike study guides, workbooks, and practice tests provided by the texbook publisher and textbook authors, *MznLnx* gives you **all** of the material in each chapter in exam form, not just samples, so you can be sure to nail your exam.

MECHANICAL

The MznLnx Exam Prep series creates exams that will help you learn the subject matter as well as test you on your understanding. Each question is designed to help you master the concept. Just working through the exams, you gain an understanding of the subject--its a simple mechanical process that produces success.

INTEGRATED STUDY GUIDE AND REVIEW

MznLnx is not just a set of exams designed to test you, its also a comprehensive review of the subject content. Each exam question is also a review of the concept, making sure that you will get the answer correct without having to go to other sources of material. You learn as you go! Its the easiest way to pass an exam.

HUMOR

Studying can be tedious and dry. MznLnx's instructional design includes moderate humor within the exam questions on occassion, to break the tedium and revitalize the brain

Chapter 1. The American Century

1. _____ is an American economist and was the Chairman of the Federal Reserve of the United States from 1987 to 2006. He currently works as a private advisor and providing consulting for firms through his company, Greenspan Associates LLC.

First appointed Federal Reserve chairman by President Ronald Reagan in August 1987, he was reappointed at successive four-year intervals until retiring on January 31, 2006 after the second-longest tenure in the position.

a. Adolph Fischer
b. Adam Smith
c. Alan Greenspan
d. Adolf Hitler

2. The _____ is a federally owned corporation in the United States created by congressional charter in May 1933 to provide navigation, flood control, electricity generation, fertilizer manufacturing, and economic development in the Tennessee Valley, a region particularly impacted by the Great Depression. The _____ was envisioned not only as an electricity provider, but also as a regional economic development agency that would use federal experts and electricity to rapidly modernize the region's economy and society.

The _____'s jurisdiction covers most of Tennessee, parts of Alabama, Mississippi, and Kentucky, and small slices of Georgia, North Carolina, and Virginia.

a. 1921 recession
b. 100-year flood
c. Tennessee Valley Authority
d. 130-30 fund

3. The _____ or gross domestic income (GDI), a basic measure of an economy's economic performance, is the market value of all final goods and services produced within the borders of a nation in a year. _____ can be defined in three ways, all of which are conceptually identical. First, it is equal to the total expenditures for all final goods and services produced within the country in a stipulated period of time (usually a 365-day year.)

a. Market structure
b. Countercyclical
c. Monopolistic competition
d. Gross domestic product

4. The _____ is an international organization that oversees the global financial system by following the macroeconomic policies of its member countries, in particular those with an impact on exchange rates and the balance of payments. It is an organization formed to stabilize international exchange rates and facilitate development. It also offers financial and technical assistance to its members, making it an international lender of last resort.

a. Office of Thrift Supervision
b. ACEA agreement
c. International Monetary Fund
d. ACCRA Cost of Living Index

5. _____ was a global military conflict which involved a majority of the world's nations, including all of the great powers, organized into two opposing military alliances: the Allies and the Axis. The war involved the mobilization of over 100 million military personnel, making it the most widespread war in history. In a state of 'total war', the major participants placed their entire economic, industrial, and scientific capabilities at the service of the war effort, erasing the distinction between civilian and military resources.

a. 100-year flood
b. 1921 recession
c. 130-30 fund
d. World War II

Chapter 1. The American Century

6. _____ is an economic system in which wealth, and the means of producing wealth, are privately owned. Through _____, the land, labor, and capital are owned, operated, and traded for the purpose of generating profits, without force or fraud, by private individuals either singly or jointly, and investments, distribution, income, production, pricing and supply of goods, commodities and services are determined by voluntary private decision in a market economy. A distinguishing feature of _____ is that each person owns his or her own labor and therefore is allowed to sell the use of it to employers.
- a. Socialism for the rich and capitalism for the poor
- b. Creative capitalism
- c. Capitalism
- d. Late capitalism

7. In finance, _____ is investment originating from other countries.See Foreign direct investment.
- a. Demand side economics
- b. Preclusive purchasing
- c. Horizontal merger
- d. Foreign investment

8. _____ is a term used to describe a policy of allowing events to take their own course. The term is a French phrase literally meaning 'let do'. It is a doctrine that states that government generally should not intervene in the marketplace.
- a. Communization
- b. Heroic capitalism
- c. Theory of Productive Forces
- d. Laissez-faire

9. _____ is a misspelled phrase from Latin 'pro capite' phrase meaning per head with pro meaning 'per' or 'for each' and capite meaning 'head.' Both words together equate to the phrase 'for each head.'

It is usually used in the field of statistics to indicate the average per person for any given concern, such as income, crime rate, etc.

It is also used in wills to indicate that each of the named beneficiaries should receive, by devise or bequest, equal shares of the estate. This is in contrast to a per stirpes division, in which each branch of the inheriting family inherits an equal share of the estate.

- a. False positive rate
- b. Population statistics
- c. Sargan test
- d. Per capita

10. The _____ was a period in the late 18th and early 19th centuries when major changes in agriculture, manufacturing, mining, and transportation had a profound effect on the socioeconomic and cultural conditions in Britain. The changes subsequently spread throughout Europe, North America, and eventually the world. The onset of the _____ marked a major turning point in human society; almost every aspect of daily life was eventually influenced in some way.
- a. Industrial Revolution
- b. Adam Smith
- c. Adolph Fischer
- d. Adolf Hitler

11. _____ was a survey conducted by the U.S. Department of Justice to gauge the prevalence of alcohol and illegal drug use among prior arrestees. It was a reformulation of the prior Drug Use Forecasting (DUF) program, focused on five drugs in particular: cocaine, marijuana, methamphetamine, opiates, and PCP.

Participants were randomly selected from arrest records in major metropolitan areas; because no personally identifying information is taken from each record chosen, the resulting data can be correlated to arrest rates, but not to the total population of persons charged.

a. ACEA agreement
b. ACCRA Cost of Living Index
c. AD-IA Model
d. Arrestee Drug Abuse Monitoring

12. _____, originally also Bolshevists were a faction of the Marxist Russian Social Democratic Labour Party which split apart from the Menshevik faction at the Second Party Congress in 1903 and ultimately became the Communist Party of the Soviet Union. The _____ seized power in Russia during the October Revolution phase of the Russian Revolution of 1917, and founded the Soviet Union.

_____ were an organization of professional revolutionaries under a strict internal hierarchy governed by the principle of democratic centralism and quasi-military discipline, who considered themselves as a vanguard of the revolutionary proletariat.

a. Redistribution game
b. Commodity form theory
c. Real socialism
d. Bolsheviks

13. _____, 1st Baron Keynes was a renowned economist from Britain whose many ideas on economic and political theories as well as on many governments' monetary policies influenced America. He advocated a government that played an active role in the lives of people regarding business, economy, etc. In this role, the government would use fiscal measures to reduce the consequences of recessions, economic depressions and booms.

a. Adam Smith
b. Adolph Fischer
c. John Maynard Keynes
d. Adolf Hitler

14. _____ was a Scottish moral philosopher and a pioneer of political economy. One of the key figures of the Scottish Enlightenment, Smith is the author of The Theory of Moral Sentiments and An Inquiry into the Nature and Causes of the Wealth of Nations. The latter, usually abbreviated as The Wealth of Nations, is considered his magnum opus and the first modern work of economics.

a. Adolph Fischer
b. Adolf Hitler
c. Adam Smith
d. Alan Greenspan

15. The _____ was one of the peace treaties at the end of World War I. It ended the state of war between Germany and the Allied Powers. It was signed on 28 June 1919, exactly five years after the assassination of Archduke Franz Ferdinand. The other Central Powers on the German side of World War I were dealt with in separate treaties.

a. Treaty of Versailles
b. 1921 recession
c. 100-year flood
d. 130-30 fund

16. _____ the Great War, and the War to End All Wars, was a global military conflict which involved the majority of the world's great powers, organized into two opposing military alliances: the Entente Powers and the Central Powers. Over 70 million military personnel were mobilized in one of the largest wars in history. In a state of total war, the major combatants fully placed their scientific and industrial capabilities at the service of the war effort.

a. 130-30 fund
b. 100-year flood
c. 1921 recession
d. World War I

17. Preparing to rebuild the international economic system as World War II was still raging, 730 delegates from all 44 Allied nations gathered at the Mount Washington Hotel in Bretton Woods, New Hampshire, United States, for the United Nations Monetary and Financial Conference. The delegates deliberated upon and signed the _____ during the first three weeks of July 1944.

Setting up a system of rules, institutions, and procedures to regulate the international monetary system, the planners at Bretton Woods established the International Monetary Fund (IMF) and the International Bank for Reconstruction and Development (IBRD), which today is part of the World Bank Group.

- a. Land reform
- b. Dromography
- c. Bretton Woods Agreements
- d. Heavy-Chemical Industry Drive

18. The _____ of 1938 (_____, ch. 676, 52 Stat. 1060, June 25, 1938, 29 U.S.C.ch.8), also called the Wages and Hours Bill, is United States federal law that applies to employees engaged in interstate commerce or employed by an enterprise engaged in commerce or in the production of goods for commerce, unless the employer can claim an exemption from coverage.

- a. Fair Labor Standards Act
- b. Generalized System of Preferences
- c. Habitability
- d. Hostile work environment

19. _____ was an Austrian-born German politician and the leader of the National Socialist German Workers Party , popularly known as the Nazi Party. He was the ruler of Germany from 1933 to 1945, serving as chancellor from 1933 to 1945 and as head of state (Führer und Reichskanzler) from 1934 to 1945.

A decorated veteran of World War I, Hitler joined the Nazi Party in 1920 and became its leader in 1921.

- a. Alan Greenspan
- b. Adolf Hitler
- c. Adolph Fischer
- d. Adam Smith

20. _____ and Keynesian Theory) is a macroeconomic theory based on the ideas of 20th-century British economist John Maynard Keynes. _____ argues that private sector decisions sometimes lead to inefficient macroeconomic outcomes and therefore advocates active policy responses by the public sector, including monetary policy actions by the central bank and fiscal policy actions by the government to stabilize output over the business cycle.

The theories forming the basis of _____ were first presented in The General Theory of Employment, Interest and Money, published in 1936.

- a. Rational choice theory
- b. Keynesian economics
- c. Deflation
- d. Market failure

21. _____s is the social science that studies the production, distribution, and consumption of goods and services. The term _____s comes from the Ancient Greek oá¼°κονομῖα from oá¼¶κος (oikos, 'house') + vĭŒµος (nomos, 'custom' or 'law'), hence 'rules of the house(hold)'. Current _____ models developed out of the broader field of political economy in the late 19th century, owing to a desire to use an empirical approach more akin to the physical sciences.

- a. Inflation
- b. Opportunity cost
- c. Economic
- d. Energy economics

22. In finance, the _____s between two currencies specifies how much one currency is worth in terms of the other. It is the value of a foreign natione;s currency in terms of the home natione;s currency. For example an _____ of 102 Japanese yen to the United States dollar means that JPY 102 is worth the same as USD 1.

a. ACEA agreement
b. ACCRA Cost of Living Index
c. Interbank market
d. Exchange rate

23. _____ comprises a radical and authoritarian nationalist political ideology and a corporatist economic ideology. Fascists advocate the creation of a single-party state. Fascists believe that nations and/or races are in perpetual conflict whereby only the strong can survive by being healthy, vital, and by asserting themselves in combat against the weak.
   a. Classical liberalism
   b. Value of Earth
   c. Third camp
   d. Fascism

24. The _____ is a monetary system in which a region's common medium of exchange are paper notes that are normally freely convertible into pre-set, fixed quantities of gold. The _____ is not currently used by any government, having been replaced completely by fiat currency. Gold certificates were used as paper currency in the United States from 1882 to 1933, these certificates were freely convertable into gold coins.

In the 1790s Britain suffered a massive shortage of silver coinage and ceased to mint larger silver coins.

   a. 100-year flood
   b. 130-30 fund
   c. 1921 recession
   d. Gold standard

25. The General Agreement on Tariffs and Trade was the outcome of the failure of negotiating governments to create the International Trade Organization (ITO.) _____ was formed in 1947 and lasted until 1994, when it was replaced by the World Trade Organization. The Bretton Woods Conference had introduced the idea for an organization to regulate trade as part of a larger plan for economic recovery after World War II.
   a. Dutch-Scandinavian Economic Pact
   b. General Agreement on Trade in Services
   c. General Agreement on Tariffs and Trade
   d. GATT

26. The _____ was the outcome of the failure of negotiating governments to create the International Trade Organization (ITO.) GATT was formed in 1947 and lasted until 1994, when it was replaced by the World Trade Organization. The Bretton Woods Conference had introduced the idea for an organization to regulate trade as part of a larger plan for economic recovery after World War II.
   a. General Agreement on Trade in Services
   b. General Agreement on Tariffs and Trade
   c. GATT
   d. Dutch-Scandinavian Economic Pact

27. A _____ is a duty imposed on goods when they are moved across a political boundary. They are usually associated with protectionism, the economic policy of restraining trade between nations. For political reasons, _____s are usually imposed on imported goods, although they may also be imposed on exported goods.
   a. Tariff
   b. 100-year flood
   c. 1921 recession
   d. 130-30 fund

28. The _____ is an international financial institution that provides financial and technical assistance to developing countries for development programs (e.g. bridges, roads, schools, etc.) with the stated goal of reducing poverty.

The _____ differs from the _____ Group, in that the _____ comprises only two institutions:

- International Bank for Reconstruction and Development (IBRD)
- International Development Association (IDA)

Whereas the latter incorporates these two in addition to three more:

- International Finance Corporation (IFC)
- Multilateral Investment Guarantee Agency (MIGA)
- International Centre for Settlement of Investment Disputes (ICSID)

John Maynard Keynes (right) represented the UK at the conference, and Harry Dexter White represented the US.

The _____ is one of two major financial institutions created as a result of the Bretton Woods Conference in 1944. The International Monetary Fund, a related but separate institution, is the second.

a. Bank-State-Branch
b. World Bank
c. Flow to Equity-Approach
d. Financial costs of the 2003 Iraq War

29. _____: Kritik der politischen Ökonomie is an extensive treatise on political economy written in German by Karl Marx and edited in part by Friedrich Engels. The book is a critical analysis of capitalism. Its first volume was published in 1867.
a. Das Kapital
b. Productive force
c. Dialectics of Nature
d. Capital accumulation

30. _____ is the building and maintaining of colonies in one territory by people from another territory. Sovereignty over the colony is claimed by the metropole. Social structure, government and economics within the territory of the colony are changed by the colonists.
a. 1921 recession
b. 130-30 fund
c. 100-year flood
d. Colonialism

31. A _____ provision refers to any program which seeks to provide a minimum level of income, service or other support for many marginalized groups such as the poor, elderly, and disabled people. _____ programs are undertaken by governments as well as non-governmental organizations (NGOs.) _____ payments and services are typically provided at the expense of taxpayers generally, funded by benefactors, or by compulsory enrollment of the poor themselves.
a. 1921 recession
b. Social welfare
c. 100-year flood
d. 130-30 fund

32. _____, refers either to the combination of a capitalist economic system with a welfare state or in a strictly American context to the practice of businesses providing welfare-like services to employees. _____ in this second sense was centered in high wage industries (not in the industries characterized by low pay, high turnover, child labor, or dangerous working conditions.) Many companies started offering higher pay and non-monetary compensation such as health care, housing, and pensions, as well as employment bureaus, in-house training, sports teams and social clubs.

Chapter 1. The American Century

a. Regional Dummy
b. Goldilocks economy
c. National savings
d. Welfare capitalism

33. _____ was a predominant American integrated oil producing, transporting, refining, and marketing company. Established in 1870 as an Ohio Corporation, it was the largest oil refiner in the world and operated as a major company trust and was one of the world's first and largest multinational corporations until it was broken up by the United States Supreme Court in 1911. John D. Rockefeller was a founder, chairman and major shareholder, and the company made him a billionaire and eventually the richest man in history.

a. 130-30 fund
b. 100-year flood
c. 1921 recession
d. Standard Oil

34. _____ is a term that is used to describe the overall process of invention, innovation and diffusion of technology or processes. The term is redundant with technological development, technological achievement, and technological progress. In essence _____ is the invention of a technology (or a process), the continuous process of improving a technology (in which it often becomes cheaper) and its diffusion throughout industry or society.

a. Technological change
b. 100-year flood
c. 1921 recession
d. 130-30 fund

35. The _____ , 1949-1991, was an economic organization of communist states and a kind of Eastern Bloc equivalent to--but more geographically inclusive than--the European Economic Community. The military equivalent to the Comecon was the Warsaw Pact, though Comecon's membership was significantly wider. The Comecon was the Eastern Bloc's reply to the formation of the OEEC .

a. 130-30 fund
b. 100-year flood
c. 1921 recession
d. Council for Mutual Economic Assistance

36. _____ is a socioeconomic structure and political ideology that promotes the establishment of an egalitarian, classless, stateless society based on common ownership and control of the means of production and property in general. In political science, the term '_____' is sometimes used to refer to communist states, a form of government in which the state operates under a one-party system and declares allegiance to Marxism-Leninism or a derivative thereof, even if the party does not actually claim that it has already reached _____.

Forerunners of communist ideas existed in antiquity and particularly in the 18th and early 19th century France, with thinkers such as Jean-Jacques Rousseau and the more radical Gracchus Babeuf.

a. Democratic centralism
b. New Communist Movement
c. Social fascism
d. Communism

37. _____ in political thought refers to economic theories of social organization advocating collective ownership and administration of the means of production and distribution of goods, and a society characterized by equality for all individuals, with an egalitarian method of compensation. Modern _____ originated in the late 19th-century intellectual and working class political movement that criticized the effects of industrialization and private ownership on society. Karl Marx posited that _____ would be achieved via class struggle and a proletarian revolution after a transitional stage from capitalism called the dictatorship of the proletariat.

a. Adam Smith
b. Adolph Fischer
c. Socialism
d. Adolf Hitler

Chapter 1. The American Century

38. The _____ is an economic and political union of 27 member states, located primarily in Europe. It was established by the Treaty of Maastricht on 1 November 1993, upon the foundations of the pre-existing European Economic Community. With a population of almost 500 million, the _____ generates an estimated 30% share (US$18.4 trillion in 2008) of the nominal gross world product.
   a. ACCRA Cost of Living Index
   b. European Union
   c. ACEA agreement
   d. European Court of Justice

39. _____ is a type of trade policy that allows traders to act and transact without interference from government. Thus, the policy permits trading partners mutual gains from trade, with goods and services produced according to the theory of comparative advantage.

Under a _____ policy, prices are a reflection of true supply and demand, and are the sole determinant of resource allocation.

   a. 100-year flood
   b. 130-30 fund
   c. 1921 recession
   d. Free Trade

40. _____ is a Regional Trade Agreement among Argentina, Brazil, Paraguay and Uruguay founded in 1991 by the Treaty of Asunci>ón, which was later amended and updated by the 1994 Treaty of Ouro Preto. Its purpose is to promote free trade and the fluid movement of goods, people, and currency.

_____ origins trace back to 1985 when Presidents Ra>úl Alfons>ín of Argentina and Jos>é Sarney of Brazil signed the Argentina-Brazil Integration and Economics Cooperation Program or PICE.

   a. 100-year flood
   b. MERCOSUR
   c. 130-30 fund
   d. Free trade area

41. The _____ is a trilateral trade bloc in North America created by the governments of the United States, Canada, and Mexico. The agreement creating the trade bloc came into force on January 1, 1994. It superseded the Canada-United States Free Trade Agreement between the U.S. and Canada.
   a. Federal Reserve Bank Notes
   b. Demand-side technologies
   c. North American Free Trade Agreement
   d. Case-Shiller Home Price Indices

42. A _____ is a free trade area with a common external tariff. The participant countries set up common external trade policy, but in some cases they use different import quotas. Common competition policy is also helpful to avoid competition deficiency.
   a. Common market
   b. Customs union
   c. Bilateral Investment Treaty
   d. Grey market

43. _____ is the shortage of common things such as food, clothing, shelter and safe drinking water, all of which determine the quality of life. It may also include the lack of access to opportunities such as education and employment which aid the escape from _____ and/or allow one to enjoy the respect of fellow citizens. According to Mollie Orshansky who developed the _____ measurements used by the U.S. government, 'to be poor is to be deprived of those goods and services and pleasures which others around us take for granted.' Ongoing debates over causes, effects and best ways to measure _____, directly influence the design and implementation of _____-reduction programs and are therefore relevant to the fields of public administration and international development.

Chapter 1. The American Century

a. Poverty map
c. Growth Elasticity of Poverty
b. Liberal welfare reforms
d. Poverty

44. A _____ or labor union is an organization of workers who have banded together to achieve common goals in key areas and working conditions. The _____, through its leadership, bargains with the employer on behalf of union members (rank and file members) and negotiates labor contracts (Collective bargaining) with employers. This may include the negotiation of wages, work rules, complaint procedures, rules governing hiring, firing and promotion of workers, benefits, workplace safety and policies.
   a. Trade union
   c. Case-Shiller Home Price Indices
   b. Guaranteed investment contracts
   d. Consumer goods

45. The _____, published in 1998 (with an epilogue added to the 1999 paperback edition), is a book by David Landes, currently Emeritus Professor of Economics and former Coolidge Professor of History at Harvard University. In it, Landes explains the 'European Miracle', or why European societies experienced a period of explosive growth when the rest of the world did not.

In doing so, he revives, at least in part, several theories he believes have been unfairly discarded by academics over the last 40 years.

   a. Wealth and poverty of nations
   c. Human Action
   b. The General Theory of Employment, Interest and Money
   d. Banks and Politics in America

46. A _____ describes one of a number of pieces of legislation relating to the reduction of smog and air pollution in general. The use by governments to enforce clean air standards has contributed to an improvement in human health and longer life spans. Critics argue it has also sapped corporate profits and contributed to outsourcing, while defenders counter that improved environmental air quality has generated more jobs than it has eliminated.
   a. Smog
   c. 100-year flood
   b. 130-30 fund
   d. Clean Air Act

47. The _____ is a United States federal law that requires the Environmental Protection Agency (EPA) to develop and enforce regulations to protect the general public from exposure to airborne contaminants that are known to be hazardous to human health. This law is an amendment to the Clean Air Act (CAA) originally passed in 1963.
   a. Meat Inspection Act
   c. Clean Air Act Extension of 1970
   b. Beneficial ownership
   d. Competition law

48. _____ changed the course of Western civilization by initiating the Protestant Reformation. As a priest and theology professor, he confronted indulgence salesmen with his 95 Theses in 1517. Luther strongly disputed their claim that freedom from God's punishment of sin could be purchased with money.
   a. Martin Luther
   c. Maximilian Carl Emil Weber
   b. Henry Ford
   d. George Cabot Lodge II

49. _____ is a movement within Christianity that originated in the sixteenth-century Protestant Reformation. It is considered to be one of the principal traditions within Christianity, together with Roman Catholicism and Eastern Orthodoxy. Anglicanism and Nontrinitarian Christianity, both of which are significantly influenced by _____, are also sometimes considered separate traditions.

a. 130-30 fund
b. 1921 recession
c. 100-year flood
d. Protestantism

50. A _____ is a system of politics and government. It is usually compared to the law system, economic system, cultural system, and other social systems. It is different from them, and can be generally defined on a spectrum from left, e.g. communism, to the right, e.g. fascism.
   a. 100-year flood
   b. 1921 recession
   c. 130-30 fund
   d. Political system

51. _____ , officially the Islamic Republic of _____, is a landlocked country that is located approximately in the center of Asia. It is variously designated as geographically located within Central Asia, South Asia, and the Middle East. It is bordered by Pakistan in the south and east, Iran in the south and west, Turkmenistan, Uzbekistan and Tajikistan in the north, and China in the far northeast.
   a. AD-IA Model
   b. ACEA agreement
   c. ACCRA Cost of Living Index
   d. Afghanistan

Chapter 2. Capitalism as an Economic System 11

1. _____ is an economic system in which wealth, and the means of producing wealth, are privately owned. Through _____, the land, labor, and capital are owned, operated, and traded for the purpose of generating profits, without force or fraud, by private individuals either singly or jointly, and investments, distribution, income, production, pricing and supply of goods, commodities and services are determined by voluntary private decision in a market economy. A distinguishing feature of _____ is that each person owns his or her own labor and therefore is allowed to sell the use of it to employers.

   a. Late capitalism
   b. Socialism for the rich and capitalism for the poor
   c. Capitalism
   d. Creative capitalism

2. The Great Proletarian _____ in the People's Republic of China was a period of widespread social and political upheaval; the nation-wide chaos and economic disarray engulfed much of Chinese society between 1966 and 1976.

It was launched by Mao Zedong, the chairman of the Communist Party of China, on May 16, 1966, who alleged that liberal bourgeoisie elements were dominating the party and insisted that they needed to be removed through post-revolutionary class struggle by mobilizing the thoughts and actions of China's youth, who formed Red Guards groups around the country. Although Mao himself officially declared the _____ to have ended in 1969, today it is widely believed that the power struggles and political instability between 1969 and the arrest of the Gang of Four as well as the death of Mao in 1976 were also part of the Revolution.

   a. 1921 recession
   b. 130-30 fund
   c. Cultural Revolution
   d. 100-year flood

3. _____ is a socioeconomic structure and political ideology that promotes the establishment of an egalitarian, classless, stateless society based on common ownership and control of the means of production and property in general. In political science, the term '_____' is sometimes used to refer to communist states, a form of government in which the state operates under a one-party system and declares allegiance to Marxism-Leninism or a derivative thereof, even if the party does not actually claim that it has already reached _____.

Forerunners of communist ideas existed in antiquity and particularly in the 18th and early 19th century France, with thinkers such as Jean-Jacques Rousseau and the more radical Gracchus Babeuf.

   a. New Communist Movement
   b. Social fascism
   c. Democratic centralism
   d. Communism

4. _____s is the social science that studies the production, distribution, and consumption of goods and services. The term _____s comes from the Ancient Greek οἰκονομία from οἶκος (oikos, 'house') + νόμος (nomos, 'custom' or 'law'), hence 'rules of the house(hold)'. Current _____ models developed out of the broader field of political economy in the late 19th century, owing to a desire to use an empirical approach more akin to the physical sciences.

   a. Opportunity cost
   b. Energy economics
   c. Inflation
   d. Economic

5. _____ is a term used to describe a policy of allowing events to take their own course. The term is a French phrase literally meaning 'let do'. It is a doctrine that states that government generally should not intervene in the marketplace.

   a. Heroic capitalism
   b. Theory of Productive Forces
   c. Communization
   d. Laissez-faire

Chapter 2. Capitalism as an Economic System

6. A _____ is the exclusive authority to determine how a resource is used, whether that resource is owned by government or by individuals. All economic goods have a _____s attribute. This attribute has three broad components

   1. The right to use the good
   2. The right to earn income from the good
   3. The right to transfer the good to others

The concept of _____s as used by economists and legal scholars are related but distinct. The distinction is largely seen in the economists' focus on the ability of an individual or collective to control the use of the good.

   a. Post-sale restraint
   b. High-reeve
   c. Holder in due course
   d. Property right

7. _____: Kritik der politischen Ökonomie is an extensive treatise on political economy written in German by Karl Marx and edited in part by Friedrich Engels. The book is a critical analysis of capitalism. Its first volume was published in 1867.
   a. Productive force
   b. Dialectics of Nature
   c. Capital accumulation
   d. Das Kapital

8. Economics:

   - _____, the desire to own something and the ability to pay for it
   - _____ curve, a graphic representation of a _____ schedule
   - _____ deposit, the money in checking accounts
   - _____ pull theory, the theory that inflation occurs when _____ for goods and services exceeds existing supplies
   - _____ schedule, a table that lists the quantity of a good a person will buy it each different price
   - _____ side economics, the school of economics at believes government spending and tax cuts open economy by raising _____

   a. McKesson ' Robbins scandal
   b. Variability
   c. Production
   d. Demand

9. _____ in economics and business is the result of an exchange and from that trade we assign a numerical monetary value to a good, service or asset. If Alice trades Bob 4 apples for an orange, the _____ of an orange is 4 apples. Inversely, the _____ of an apple is 1/4 oranges.
   a. Price
   b. Premium pricing
   c. Price book
   d. Price war

10. A _____ or market-based mechanism is any of a wide variety of ways to match up buyers and sellers.

An example of a _____ uses announced bid and ask prices. Generally speaking, when two parties wish to engage in a trade, the purchaser will announce a price he is willing to pay (the bid price) and seller will announce a price he is willing to accept (the ask price.)

Chapter 2. Capitalism as an Economic System

a. Horizontal market
b. Price mechanism
c. Marketization
d. Market equilibrium

11. In economics, a _____ is any economic system that effects its distribution of goods and services with prices and employing any form of money or debt tokens. Except for possible remote and primitive communities, all modern societies use _____s to allocate resources. However, _____s are not used for all resource allocation decisions today.
   a. Hanseatic League
   b. Family economy
   c. Neomercantilism
   d. Price system

12. _____ is an economic model based on price, utility and quantity in a market. It predicts that in a competitive market, price will function to equalize the quantity demanded by consumers, and the quantity supplied by producers, resulting in an economic equilibrium of price and quantity. The model incorporates other factors changing equilibrium as a shift of demand and/or supply.
   a. Joint demand
   b. Rational addiction
   c. Supply and demand
   d. Deferred gratification

13. _____ was a survey conducted by the U.S. Department of Justice to gauge the prevalence of alcohol and illegal drug use among prior arrestees. It was a reformulation of the prior Drug Use Forecasting (DUF) program, focused on five drugs in particular: cocaine, marijuana, methamphetamine, opiates, and PCP.

Participants were randomly selected from arrest records in major metropolitan areas; because no personally identifying information is taken from each record chosen, the resulting data can be correlated to arrest rates, but not to the total population of persons charged.

   a. Arrestee Drug Abuse Monitoring
   b. AD-IA Model
   c. ACCRA Cost of Living Index
   d. ACEA agreement

14. A political party described as a _____ includes those that advocate the application of the social principles of communism through a communist form of government. The name originates from the 1848 tract Manifesto of the _____ by Karl Marx, Friedrich Engels. The Leninist concept of a _____ encompasses a larger political system and includes not only an ideological orientation but also a wide set of organizational policies.
   a. Criticisms of Communist party rule
   b. Communism
   c. Communist Party
   d. Criticisms of anarcho-capitalism

15. _____ was a Scottish moral philosopher and a pioneer of political economy. One of the key figures of the Scottish Enlightenment, Smith is the author of The Theory of Moral Sentiments and An Inquiry into the Nature and Causes of the Wealth of Nations. The latter, usually abbreviated as The Wealth of Nations, is considered his magnum opus and the first modern work of economics.
   a. Adolph Fischer
   b. Alan Greenspan
   c. Adolf Hitler
   d. Adam Smith

Chapter 2. Capitalism as an Economic System

16. _____ is an economic theory that holds that the prosperity of a nation is dependent upon its supply of capital, and that the global volume of international trade is 'unchangeable.' Economic assets or capital, are represented by bullion (gold, silver, and trade value) held by the state, which is best increased through a positive balance of trade with other nations (exports minus imports.) _____ suggests that the ruling government should advance these goals by playing a protectionist role in the economy; by encouraging exports and discouraging imports, notably through the use of tariffs and subsidies.

_____ was the dominant school of thought throughout the early modern period (from the 16th to the 18th century.)

- a. General equilibrium theory
- b. Consumer theory
- c. Mercantilism
- d. Nominal value

17. _____ refers to various ideologies based on a concept that competition among all individuals, groups, nations, or ideas drives social evolution in human societies. The term draws upon the common use of the term Darwinism, which is a social adaptation of the theory of natural selection as first advanced by Charles Darwin. Natural selection explains speciation in populations as the outcome of competition between individual organisms for limited resources or 'survival of the fittest' (a term in fact coined by Herbert Spencer) (also refer to 'The Gospel of Wealth' theory written by Andrew Carnegie.)
- a. 130-30 fund
- b. 100-year flood
- c. 1921 recession
- d. Social Darwinism

18. _____ is a broad label that refers to any individuals or households that use goods and services generated within the economy. The concept of a _____ is used in different contexts, so that the usage and significance of the term may vary.

Typically when business people and economists talk of _____s they are talking about person as _____, an aggregated commodity item with little individuality other than that expressed in the buy/not-buy decision.

- a. 1921 recession
- b. 130-30 fund
- c. 100-year flood
- d. Consumer

19. The _____, sometimes called the Puritan Work Ethic, is a sociological, theoretical concept. It is based upon the notion that the Calvinist emphasis on the necessity for hard work is proponent of a person's calling and worldly success is a sign of personal salvation. It is argued that Protestants beginning with Martin Luther had reconceptualised worldly work as a duty which benefits both the individual and society as a whole.
- a. 130-30 fund
- b. 100-year flood
- c. 1921 recession
- d. Protestant work ethic

20. _____ is Latin for 'Let the buyer beware'. Generally _____ is the property law doctrine that controls the sale of real property after the date of closing.

Under the doctrine of _____, the buyer could not recover from the seller for defects on the property that rendered the property unfit for ordinary purposes.

a. 1921 recession
b. 100-year flood
c. 130-30 fund
d. Caveat emptor

21. _____ is a term which is used in economics to refer to the rule or sovereignty of purchasers in markets as to production of goods. It is the power of consumers to decide what gets produced. People use the this term to describe the consumer as the 'king,' or ruler, of the market, the one who determines what products will be produced.
   a. Schedule delay
   b. Reservation price
   c. Microeconomic reform
   d. Consumer sovereignty

22. _____ was an American industrialist and philanthropist. Rockefeller revolutionized the petroleum industry and defined the structure of modern philanthropy. In 1870, he founded the Standard Oil Company and ran it until he officially retired in 1897.
   a. John Davison Rockefeller
   b. Adolph Fischer
   c. Adam Smith
   d. Adolf Hitler

23. _____ is a government outline where any more than minimal governmental intervention in personal liberties and the economy is not usually allowed by law, usually in a written Constitution. It is closely related to libertarianism, classical liberalism, and some tendencies of liberalism and conservatism in the United States.

   _____ is a common practice through Western culture.

   a. 100-year flood
   b. Limited government
   c. 1921 recession
   d. 130-30 fund

24. In economics, the _____ is a graphical representation of the cumulative distribution function of a probability distribution; it is a graph showing the proportion of the distribution assumed by the bottom y% of the values. It is a curve that illustrates income distribution. It is often used to represent income distribution, where it shows for the bottom x% of households, what percentage y% of the total income they have.
   a. Phillips curve
   b. Demand curve
   c. Kuznets curve
   d. Lorenz curve

25. The _____, asbl is a non-profit project which produces a cross-national database of micro-economic income data for social science research. The project started in 1983 and is headquartered in Luxembourg. In 2006 the database included data from 30 countries on four continents, with some countries represented for over 30 years.
   a. Deutsche Bank
   b. Leading stock
   c. Bankruptcy of Lehman Brothers
   d. Luxembourg income study

26. In mathematics, a _____ is a constant multiplicative factor of a certain object. For example, in the expression $9x^2$, the _____ of x^2 is 9.

The object can be such things as a variable, a vector, a function, etc.

   a. 1921 recession
   b. 100-year flood
   c. 130-30 fund
   d. Coefficient

Chapter 2. Capitalism as an Economic System

27. In economics, _____ is how a natione;s total economy is distributed among its population. _____ has always been a central concern of economic theory and economic policy. Classical economists such as Adam Smith, Thomas Malthus and David Ricardo were mainly concerned with factor _____, that is, the distribution of income between the main factors of production, land, labour and capital.

    a. Income distribution
    b. Equipment trust certificate
    c. Eco commerce
    d. Authorised capital

28. In mathematics, an _____ is a statement about the relative size or order of two objects, or about whether they are the same or not

    - The notation a < b means that a is less than b.
    - The notation a > b means that a is greater than b.
    - The notation a ≠ b means that a is not equal to b, but does not say that one is greater than the other or even that they can be compared in size.

    In each statement above, a is not equal to b. These relations are known as strict inequalities. The notation a < b may also be read as 'a is strictly less than b'.

    a. Inequality
    b. AD-IA Model
    c. ACCRA Cost of Living Index
    d. ACEA agreement

29. The _____ is a measure of statistical dispersion, commonly used as a measure of inequality of income distribution or inequality of wealth distribution. It is defined as a ratio with values between 0 and 1: A low _____ indicates more equal income or wealth distribution, while a high _____ indicates more unequal distribution. 0 corresponds to perfect equality (everyone having exactly the same income) and 1 corresponds to perfect inequality (where one person has all the income, while everyone else has zero income.)

    a. Leapfrogging
    b. Compensating variation
    c. Suits index
    d. Gini coefficient

30. The Organisation for Economic Co-operation and Development (_____) is an international organisation of 30 countries that accept the principles of representative democracy and free-market economy. Most _____ members are high-income economies with a high HDI and are regarded as developed countries.

    It originated in 1948 as the Organisation for European Economic Co-operation, led by Robert Marjolin of France, to help administer the Marshall Plan for the reconstruction of Europe after World War II.

    a. ACEA agreement
    b. AD-IA Model
    c. OECD
    d. ACCRA Cost of Living Index

31. _____ is a type of trade policy that allows traders to act and transact without interference from government. Thus, the policy permits trading partners mutual gains from trade, with goods and services produced according to the theory of comparative advantage.

    Under a _____ policy, prices are a reflection of true supply and demand, and are the sole determinant of resource allocation.

a. 1921 recession
b. 130-30 fund
c. 100-year flood
d. Free Trade

32. The _____ is a trilateral trade bloc in North America created by the governments of the United States, Canada, and Mexico. The agreement creating the trade bloc came into force on January 1, 1994. It superseded the Canada-United States Free Trade Agreement between the U.S. and Canada.
   a. Federal Reserve Bank Notes
   b. Demand-side technologies
   c. North American Free Trade Agreement
   d. Case-Shiller Home Price Indices

33. _____ Abd al-Majid al-Tikriti was the President of Iraq from July 16, 1979 until April 9, 2003.

A leading member of the revolutionary Ba'ath Party, which espoused secular pan-Arabism, economic modernization, and Arab socialism, Saddam played a key role in the 1968 coup that brought the party to long-term power. As vice president under the ailing General Ahmed Hassan al-Bakr, Saddam tightly controlled conflict between the government and the armed forces--at a time when many other groups were considered capable of overthrowing the government--by creating repressive security forces.

   a. Adolf Hitler
   b. Adam Smith
   c. Adolph Fischer
   d. Saddam Hussein

34. _____ is a term used in national accounts statistics and macroeconomics. It basically refers to the net additions to the (physical) capital stock in an accounting period, or, to the value of the increase of the capital stock; though it may occasionally also refer to the (growth of the) total stock of capital formed.

Thus, in UNSNA, _____ equals fixed capital investment, the increase in the value of inventories held, plus (net) lending to foreign countries, during an accounting period.

   a. Capital flight
   b. Consumption of fixed capital
   c. Capital intensity
   d. Capital formation

35. The _____ is an international organization that oversees the global financial system by following the macroeconomic policies of its member countries, in particular those with an impact on exchange rates and the balance of payments. It is an organization formed to stabilize international exchange rates and facilitate development. It also offers financial and technical assistance to its members, making it an international lender of last resort.
   a. Office of Thrift Supervision
   b. ACCRA Cost of Living Index
   c. ACEA agreement
   d. International Monetary Fund

36. An _____ or Ä"conomic system is a system that involves the production, distribution and consumption of goods and services between the entities in a particular society. It is the method used by society to produce and distribute goods and services. The _____ is composed of people and institutions, including their relationships to productive resources, such as through the convention of property.
   a. Information economy
   b. Intention economy
   c. Indicative planning
   d. Economic system

Chapter 2. Capitalism as an Economic System

37. _____ is a dystopian novel by George Orwell. Published in England on 17 August 1945, the book reflects events leading up to and during the Stalin era before World War II. Orwell, a democratic socialist and a member of the Independent Labour Party for many years, was a critic of Joseph Stalin and was suspicious of Moscow-directed Stalinism after his experiences with the NKVD during the Spanish Civil War.

   a. Adolph Fischer
   b. Adam Smith
   c. Animal Farm
   d. Adolf Hitler

38. Competition law, known in the United States as _____ law, has three main elements:

   - prohibiting agreements or practices that restrict free trading and competition between business entities. This includes in particular the repression of cartels.
   - banning abusive behaviour by a firm dominating a market, or anti-competitive practices that tend to lead to such a dominant position. Practices controlled in this way may include predatory pricing, tying, price gouging, refusal to deal, and many others.
   - supervising the mergers and acquisitions of large corporations, including some joint ventures. Transactions that are considered to threaten the competitive process can be prohibited altogether, or approved subject to 'remedies' such as an obligation to divest part of the merged business or to offer licences or access to facilities to enable other businesses to continue competing.

   The substance and practice of competition law varies from jurisdiction to jurisdiction. Protecting the interests of consumers (consumer welfare) and ensuring that entrepreneurs have an opportunity to compete in the market economy are often treated as important objectives. Competition law is closely connected with law on deregulation of access to markets, state aids and subsidies, the privatisation of state owned assets and the establishment of independent sector regulators. In recent decades, competition law has been viewed as a way to provide better public services.

   a. United Kingdom competition law
   b. Intellectual property law
   c. Antitrust
   d. Anti-Inflation Act

39. _____, known in the United States as antitrust law, has three main elements:

   - prohibiting agreements or practices that restrict free trading and competition between business entities. This includes in particular the repression of cartels.
   - banning abusive behaviour by a firm dominating a market, or anti-competitive practices that tend to lead to such a dominant position. Practices controlled in this way may include predatory pricing, tying, price gouging, refusal to deal, and many others.
   - supervising the mergers and acquisitions of large corporations, including some joint ventures. Transactions that are considered to threaten the competitive process can be prohibited altogether, or approved subject to 'remedies' such as an obligation to divest part of the merged business or to offer licences or access to facilities to enable other businesses to continue competing.

The substance and practice of _____ varies from jurisdiction to jurisdiction. Protecting the interests of consumers (consumer welfare) and ensuring that entrepreneurs have an opportunity to compete in the market economy are often treated as important objectives. _____ is closely connected with law on deregulation of access to markets, state aids and subsidies, the privatisation of state owned assets and the establishment of independent sector regulators. In recent decades, _____ has been viewed as a way to provide better public services.

a. Fee simple
b. Hostile work environment
c. Due diligence
d. Competition law

40. _____ was an English philosopher. Locke is considered the first of the British empiricists, but is equally important to social contract theory. His ideas had enormous influence on the development of epistemology and political philosophy, and he is widely regarded as one of the most influential Enlightenment thinkers, classical republicans, and contributors to liberal theory.
a. 100-year flood
b. 130-30 fund
c. 1921 recession
d. John Locke

41. _____, in law and economics, is a form of risk management primarily used to hedge against the risk of a contingent loss. _____ is defined as the equitable transfer of the risk of a loss, from one entity to another, in exchange for a premium, and can be thought of as a guaranteed small loss to prevent a large, possibly devastating loss. An insurer is a company selling the _____; an insured or policyholder is the person or entity buying the _____.
a. ACEA agreement
b. Insurance
c. ACCRA Cost of Living Index
d. AD-IA Model

42. A _____ is a theoretical term that economists use to describe a market which is free from government intervention (i.e. no regulation, no subsidization, no single monetary system and no governmental monopolies.) In a _____, property rights are voluntarily exchanged at a price arranged solely by the mutual consent of sellers and buyers. By definition, buyers and sellers do not coerce each other, in the sense that they obtain each other's property without the use of physical force, threat of physical force, or fraud, nor is the coerced by a third party (such as by government via transfer payments) and they engage in trade simply because they both consent and believe that it is a good enough choice.
a. Delegation
b. Leninism
c. Third camp
d. Free market

43. A _____ is an economy based on the division of labor in which the prices of goods and services are determined in a free price system set by supply and demand. This is often contrasted with a planned economy, in which a central government determines the price of goods and services using a fixed price system. Market economies are contrasted with mixed economy where the price system is not entirely free but under some government control that is not extensive enough to constitute a planned economy.
a. Commons-based peer production
b. Nutritional Economics
c. Network Economy
d. Market economy

44. The _____ is the part of economic and administrative life that deals with the delivery of goods and services by and for the government, whether national, regional or local/municipal.

Examples of _____ activity range from delivering social security, administering urban planning and organising national defenses.

The organization of the _____ can take several forms, including:

- Direct administration funded through taxation; the delivering organization generally has no specific requirement to meet commercial success criteria, and production decisions are determined by government.
- Publicly owned corporations (in some contexts, especially manufacturing, 'state-owned enterprises'); which differ from direct administration in that they have greater commercial freedoms and are expected to operate according to commercial criteria, and production decisions are not generally taken by government (although goals may be set for them by government.)
- Partial outsourcing (of the scale many businesses do, e.g. for IT services), is considered a _____ model.

A borderline form is

- Complete outsourcing or contracting out, with a privately owned corporation delivering the entire service on behalf of government. This may be considered a mixture of private sector operations with public ownership of assets, although in some forms the private sector's control and/or risk is so great that the service may no longer be considered part of the _____.

a. Public sector
c. Policy cycle
b. 100-year flood
d. 130-30 fund

45. To _____ is to impose a financial charge or other levy upon a taxpayer by a state or the functional equivalent of a state.

_____es are also imposed by many subnational entities. _____es consist of direct _____ or indirect _____, and may be paid in money or as its labour equivalent (often but not always unpaid.)

a. Tax
c. 1921 recession
b. 100-year flood
d. 130-30 fund

46. To tax is to impose a financial charge or other levy upon a taxpayer by a state or the functional equivalent of a state.

_____ are also imposed by many subnational entities. _____ consist of direct tax or indirect tax, and may be paid in money or as its labour equivalent (often but not always unpaid.)

a. Taxes
c. 100-year flood
b. 130-30 fund
d. 1921 recession

Chapter 3. The United States

1. _____ is an economic theory that holds that the prosperity of a nation is dependent upon its supply of capital, and that the global volume of international trade is 'unchangeable.' Economic assets or capital, are represented by bullion (gold, silver, and trade value) held by the state, which is best increased through a positive balance of trade with other nations (exports minus imports.) _____ suggests that the ruling government should advance these goals by playing a protectionist role in the economy; by encouraging exports and discouraging imports, notably through the use of tariffs and subsidies.

_____ was the dominant school of thought throughout the early modern period (from the 16th to the 18th century.)

- a. Mercantilism
- b. General equilibrium theory
- c. Nominal value
- d. Consumer theory

2. A _____ describes one of a number of pieces of legislation relating to the reduction of smog and air pollution in general. The use by governments to enforce clean air standards has contributed to an improvement in human health and longer life spans. Critics argue it has also sapped corporate profits and contributed to outsourcing, while defenders counter that improved environmental air quality has generated more jobs than it has eliminated.
- a. 130-30 fund
- b. Smog
- c. 100-year flood
- d. Clean Air Act

3. The _____ is a United States federal law that requires the Environmental Protection Agency (EPA) to develop and enforce regulations to protect the general public from exposure to airborne contaminants that are known to be hazardous to human health. This law is an amendment to the Clean Air Act (CAA) originally passed in 1963.
- a. Beneficial ownership
- b. Meat Inspection Act
- c. Competition law
- d. Clean Air Act Extension of 1970

4. A political party described as a _____ includes those that advocate the application of the social principles of communism through a communist form of government. The name originates from the 1848 tract Manifesto of the _____ by Karl Marx, Friedrich Engels. The Leninist concept of a _____ encompases a larger political system and includes not only an ideological orientation but also a wide set of organizational policies.
- a. Communism
- b. Communist Party
- c. Criticisms of Communist party rule
- d. Criticisms of anarcho-capitalism

5.

_____ is, in very basic words, a position a firm occupies against its competitors.

According to Michael Porter, the three methods for creating a sustainable _____ are through:

1. Cost leadership - Cost advantage occurs when a firm delivers the same services as its competitors but at a lower cost;

2. Differentiation - Differentiation advantage occurs when a firm delivers greater services for the same price of its competitors. They are collectively known as positional advantages because they denote the firm's position in its industry as a leader in either superior services or cost;

Chapter 3. The United States

3. Focus (economics) - A focused approach requires the firm to concentrate on a narrow, exclusive competitive segment (market niche), hoping to achieve a local rather than industry wide _____. There are cost focus seekers, who aim to obtain a local cost advantage over competition and differentiation focuser, who are looking for a local difference.

- a. Competitive Advantage
- b. National Diamond
- c. Six Forces Model
- d. Chaos theory in organizational development

6. _____ is the shortage of common things such as food, clothing, shelter and safe drinking water, all of which determine the quality of life. It may also include the lack of access to opportunities such as education and employment which aid the escape from _____ and/or allow one to enjoy the respect of fellow citizens. According to Mollie Orshansky who developed the _____ measurements used by the U.S. government, 'to be poor is to be deprived of those goods and services and pleasures which others around us take for granted.' Ongoing debates over causes, effects and best ways to measure _____, directly influence the design and implementation of _____-reduction programs and are therefore relevant to the fields of public administration and international development.

- a. Liberal welfare reforms
- b. Poverty map
- c. Growth Elasticity of Poverty
- d. Poverty

7. The _____, published in 1998 (with an epilogue added to the 1999 paperback edition), is a book by David Landes, currently Emeritus Professor of Economics and former Coolidge Professor of History at Harvard University. In it, Landes explains the 'European Miracle', or why European societies experienced a period of explosive growth when the rest of the world did not.

In doing so, he revives, at least in part, several theories he believes have been unfairly discarded by academics over the last 40 years.

- a. Wealth and Poverty of Nations
- b. Human Action
- c. Banks and Politics in America
- d. The General Theory of Employment, Interest and Money

8. _____ was a global military conflict which involved a majority of the world's nations, including all of the great powers, organized into two opposing military alliances: the Allies and the Axis. The war involved the mobilization of over 100 million military personnel, making it the most widespread war in history. In a state of 'total war', the major participants placed their entire economic, industrial, and scientific capabilities at the service of the war effort, erasing the distinction between civilian and military resources.

- a. 100-year flood
- b. 1921 recession
- c. World War II
- d. 130-30 fund

9. _____ is an economic system in which wealth, and the means of producing wealth, are privately owned. Through _____, the land, labor, and capital are owned, operated, and traded for the purpose of generating profits, without force or fraud, by private individuals either singly or jointly, and investments, distribution, income, production, pricing and supply of goods, commodities and services are determined by voluntary private decision in a market economy. A distinguishing feature of _____ is that each person owns his or her own labor and therefore is allowed to sell the use of it to employers.

a. Late capitalism
b. Socialism for the rich and capitalism for the poor
c. Creative capitalism
d. Capitalism

10. _____s is the social science that studies the production, distribution, and consumption of goods and services. The term _____s comes from the Ancient Greek oá¼°κονομῖα from oá¼¶κος (oikos, 'house') + vÏŒμος (nomos, 'custom' or 'law'), hence 'rules of the house(hold)'. Current _____ models developed out of the broader field of political economy in the late 19th century, owing to a desire to use an empirical approach more akin to the physical sciences.
    a. Inflation
    b. Energy economics
    c. Opportunity cost
    d. Economic

11. _____ was a Scottish-born American industrialist, businessman, and a major philanthropist. He was an immigrant as a child with his parents. He built Pittsburgh's Carnegie Steel Company, which was later merged with Elbert H. Gary's Federal Steel Company and several smaller companies to create U.S. Steel.
    a. Eli Whitney
    b. Alfred Marshall
    c. Oskar Morgenstern
    d. Andrew Carnegie

12. _____ is a broad label that refers to any individuals or households that use goods and services generated within the economy. The concept of a _____ is used in different contexts, so that the usage and significance of the term may vary.

Typically when business people and economists talk of _____s they are talking about person as _____, an aggregated commodity item with little individuality other than that expressed in the buy/not-buy decision.

    a. Consumer
    b. 1921 recession
    c. 130-30 fund
    d. 100-year flood

13. _____ was an American industrialist and philanthropist. Rockefeller revolutionized the petroleum industry and defined the structure of modern philanthropy. In 1870, he founded the Standard Oil Company and ran it until he officially retired in 1897.
    a. Adolph Fischer
    b. Adolf Hitler
    c. John Davison Rockefeller
    d. Adam Smith

14. The _____ is the largest national economy in the world. Its gross domestic product (GDP) was estimated as $14.2 trillion in 2008. The U.S. economy maintains a high level of output per person (GDP per capita, $46,800 in 2008, ranked at around number ten in the world.)
    a. AD-IA Model
    b. ACEA agreement
    c. ACCRA Cost of Living Index
    d. Economy of the United States

15. The _____ is the central United States governmental body, established by the United States Constitution. The federal government has three branches: the legislative, executive, and judicial. Through a system of separation of powers and the system of 'checks and balances,' each of these branches has some authority to act on its own, some authority to regulate the other two branches, and has some of its own authority, in turn, regulated by the other branches.
    a. 1921 recession
    b. 130-30 fund
    c. 100-year flood
    d. Federal government of the United States

16. _____ is a common concept in economics, and gives rise to derived concepts such as consumer debt. Generally _____ is defined by opposition to production. But the precise definition can vary because different schools of economists define production quite differently.
   a. Consumption
   b. Cash or share options
   c. Federal Reserve Bank Notes
   d. Foreclosure data providers

17. _____ in economics and business is the result of an exchange and from that trade we assign a numerical monetary value to a good, service or asset. If Alice trades Bob 4 apples for an orange, the _____ of an orange is 4 apples. Inversely, the _____ of an apple is 1/4 oranges.
   a. Price
   b. Premium pricing
   c. Price book
   d. Price war

18. A _____ or market-based mechanism is any of a wide variety of ways to match up buyers and sellers.

An example of a _____ uses announced bid and ask prices. Generally speaking, when two parties wish to engage in a trade, the purchaser will announce a price he is willing to pay (the bid price) and seller will announce a price he is willing to accept (the ask price.)

   a. Horizontal market
   b. Marketization
   c. Price mechanism
   d. Market equilibrium

19. _____ is a term that is used to describe the overall process of invention, innovation and diffusion of technology or processes. The term is redundant with technological development, technological achievement, and technological progress. In essence _____ is the invention of a technology (or a process), the continuous process of improving a technology (in which it often becomes cheaper) and its diffusion throughout industry or society.
   a. 1921 recession
   b. 100-year flood
   c. 130-30 fund
   d. Technological change

20. _____ was a survey conducted by the U.S. Department of Justice to gauge the prevalence of alcohol and illegal drug use among prior arrestees. It was a reformulation of the prior Drug Use Forecasting (DUF) program, focused on five drugs in particular: cocaine, marijuana, methamphetamine, opiates, and PCP.

Participants were randomly selected from arrest records in major metropolitan areas; because no personally identifying information is taken from each record chosen, the resulting data can be correlated to arrest rates, but not to the total population of persons charged.

   a. ACCRA Cost of Living Index
   b. ACEA agreement
   c. AD-IA Model
   d. Arrestee Drug Abuse Monitoring

21. The _____ of 1938 (_____, ch. 676, 52 Stat. 1060, June 25, 1938, 29 U.S.C.ch.8), also called the Wages and Hours Bill, is United States federal law that applies to employees engaged in interstate commerce or employed by an enterprise engaged in commerce or in the production of goods for commerce, unless the employer can claim an exemption from coverage.
   a. Fair Labor Standards Act
   b. Generalized System of Preferences
   c. Habitability
   d. Hostile work environment

Chapter 3. The United States

22. _____ was a Scottish moral philosopher and a pioneer of political economy. One of the key figures of the Scottish Enlightenment, Smith is the author of The Theory of Moral Sentiments and An Inquiry into the Nature and Causes of the Wealth of Nations. The latter, usually abbreviated as The Wealth of Nations, is considered his magnum opus and the first modern work of economics.
- a. Adolf Hitler
- b. Adolph Fischer
- c. Alan Greenspan
- d. Adam Smith

23. _____ laws are designed to ensure fair competition and the free flow of truthful information in the marketplace. The laws are designed to prevent businesses that engage in fraud or specified unfair practices from gaining an advantage over competitors and may provide additional protection for the weak and unable to take care of themselves. _____ laws are a form of government regulation which protects the interests of consumers.
- a. History of minimum wage
- b. Dow Jones Industrial Average
- c. Global warming
- d. Consumer protection

24. _____ is that which is owed; usually referencing assets owed, but the term can also cover moral obligations and other interactions not requiring money. In the case of assets, _____ is a means of using future purchasing power in the present before a summation has been earned. Some companies and corporations use _____ as a part of their overall corporate finance strategy.
- a. Collateral Management
- b. Hard money loan
- c. Debt
- d. Debenture

25. _____, in law and economics, is a form of risk management primarily used to hedge against the risk of a contingent loss. _____ is defined as the equitable transfer of the risk of a loss, from one entity to another, in exchange for a premium, and can be thought of as a guaranteed small loss to prevent a large, possibly devastating loss. An insurer is a company selling the _____; an insured or policyholder is the person or entity buying the _____.
- a. ACEA agreement
- b. ACCRA Cost of Living Index
- c. AD-IA Model
- d. Insurance

26. In general, a _____ is an arrangement to provide people with an income when they are no longer earning a regular income from employment.

The terms retirement plan or superannuation refer to a _____ granted upon retirement . Retirement plans may be set up by employers, insurance companies, the government or other institutions such as employer associations or trade unions.
- a. Pension
- b. Real wage
- c. Superannuation
- d. Profit-sharing agreement

27. A _____ is the procedure of systematically acquiring and recording information about the members of a given population. It is a regularly occurring and official count of a particular population. The term is used mostly in connection with national 'population and door to door _____es' (to be taken every 10 years according to United Nations recommendations), agriculture, and business _____es.
- a. 130-30 fund
- b. 1921 recession
- c. 100-year flood
- d. Census

Chapter 3. The United States

28. The _____ was a landmark piece of legislation in the United States that outlawed racial segregation in schools, public places, and employment.
   a. Civil Rights Act of 1964
   b. Postcautionary principle
   c. Patent portfolio
   d. Le Chapelier Law

29. The _____ established the Federal Deposit Insurance Corporation (FDIC) in the United States and included banking reforms, some of which were designed to control speculation. Some provisions such as Regulation Q, which allowed the Federal Reserve to regulate interest rates in savings accounts, were repealed by the Depository Institutions Deregulation and Monetary Control Act of 1980. Provisions that prohibit a bank holding company from owning other financial companies were repealed on November 12, 1999, by the Gramm-Leach-Bliley Act.
   a. 1921 recession
   b. Glass-Steagall Act of 1933
   c. 100-year flood
   d. 130-30 fund

30. In business and accounting, _____ are everything of value that is owned by a person or company. It is a claim on the property your income of a borrower. The balance sheet of a firm records the monetary value of the _____ owned by the firm.
   a. Amortization schedule
   b. ACEA agreement
   c. ACCRA Cost of Living Index
   d. Assets

31. The _____ consists of a number of economic theories which describe the nature of the firm, company including its existence, its behaviour, and its relationship with the market.

In simplified terms, the _____ aims to answer these questions:

1. Existence - why do firms emerge, why are not all transactions in the economy mediated over the market?
2. Boundaries - why the boundary between firms and the market is located exactly there? Which transactions are performed internally and which are negotiated on the market?
3. Organization - why are firms structured in such specific way? What is the interplay of formal and informal relationships?

Despite looking simple, these questions are not answered by the established economic theory, which usually views firms as given, and treats them as black boxes without any internal structure.

The First World War period saw a change of emphasis in economic theory away from industry-level analysis which mainly included analysing markets to analysis at the level of the firm, as it became increasingly clear that perfect competition was no longer an adequate model of how firms behaved. Economic theory till then had focussed on trying to understand markets alone and there had been little study on understanding why firms or organisations exist.

   a. Theory of the firm
   b. Khazzoom-Brookes postulate
   c. Technology gap
   d. Policy Ineffectiveness Proposition

32. _____ in its literal sense is the process of transformation of local or regional phenomena into global ones. It can be described as a process by which the people of the world are unified into a single society and function together.

Chapter 3. The United States

This process is a combination of economic, technological, sociocultural and political forces.

a. Helsinki Process on Globalisation and Democracy
b. Globally Integrated Enterprise
c. Global Cosmopolitanism
d. Globalization

33. The phrase _____ and acquisitions refers to the aspect of corporate strategy, corporate finance and management dealing with the buying, selling and combining of different companies that can aid, finance, or help a growing company in a given industry grow rapidly without having to create another business entity.

An acquisition, also known as a takeover or a buyout, is the buying of one company (the 'target') by another. An acquisition may be friendly or hostile.

a. Differential accumulation
b. Peace dividend
c. Political economy
d. Mergers

34. The term _____ used by politicians and economists to measure broader social effects of policies, such as the effect that reducing graffiti or vandalism might have on the wellbeing of local residents.

Two widely known measures of a country's liveability are the Economist Intelligence Unit's _____ index and the Mercer Quality of Living Survey. Both measures calculate the liveability of countries around the world through a combination of subjective life-satisfaction surveys and objective determinants of _____ such as divorce rates, safety, and infrastructure.

a. Compliance cost
b. Genuine progress indicator
c. Culture of capitalism
d. Quality of life

35. A _____ is a business that is privately owned and operated, with a small number of employees and relatively low volume of sales. The legal definition of 'small' often varies by country and industry, but is generally under 100 employees in the United States and under 50 employees in the European Union. In comparison, the definition of mid-sized business by the number of employees is generally under 500 in the U.S. and 250 for the European Union.

a. Procurement
b. Small Business
c. Cabotage
d. Farmshoring

36. A _____ or labor union is an organization of workers who have banded together to achieve common goals in key areas and working conditions. The _____, through its leadership, bargains with the employer on behalf of union members (rank and file members) and negotiates labor contracts (Collective bargaining) with employers. This may include the negotiation of wages, work rules, complaint procedures, rules governing hiring, firing and promotion of workers, benefits, workplace safety and policies.

a. Trade union
b. Case-Shiller Home Price Indices
c. Consumer goods
d. Guaranteed investment contracts

37. In mathematics, a _____ is a constant multiplicative factor of a certain object. For example, in the expression $9x^2$, the _____ of x^2 is 9.

The object can be such things as a variable, a vector, a function, etc.

Chapter 3. The United States

a. 1921 recession
b. 130-30 fund
c. 100-year flood
d. Coefficient

38. In a company, _____ is the sum of all financial records of salaries, wages, bonuses and deductions.

A paycheck, is traditionally a paper document issued by an employer to pay an employee for services rendered. While most commonly used in the United States, recently the physical paycheck has been increasingly replaced by electronic direct deposit to bank accounts.

a. Total Expense Ratio
b. Tax expense
c. 100-year flood
d. Payroll

39. The Great Proletarian _____ in the People's Republic of China was a period of widespread social and political upheaval; the nation-wide chaos and economic disarray engulfed much of Chinese society between 1966 and 1976.

It was launched by Mao Zedong, the chairman of the Communist Party of China, on May 16, 1966, who alleged that liberal bourgeoisie elements were dominating the party and insisted that they needed to be removed through post-revolutionary class struggle by mobilizing the thoughts and actions of China's youth, who formed Red Guards groups around the country. Although Mao himself officially declared the _____ to have ended in 1969, today it is widely believed that the power struggles and political instability between 1969 and the arrest of the Gang of Four as well as the death of Mao in 1976 were also part of the Revolution.

a. 130-30 fund
b. 100-year flood
c. Cultural Revolution
d. 1921 recession

40. _____ Abd al-Majid al-Tikriti was the President of Iraq from July 16, 1979 until April 9, 2003.

A leading member of the revolutionary Ba'ath Party, which espoused secular pan-Arabism, economic modernization, and Arab socialism, Saddam played a key role in the 1968 coup that brought the party to long-term power. As vice president under the ailing General Ahmed Hassan al-Bakr, Saddam tightly controlled conflict between the government and the armed forces--at a time when many other groups were considered capable of overthrowing the government--by creating repressive security forces.

a. Adam Smith
b. Adolf Hitler
c. Adolph Fischer
d. Saddam Hussein

41. An _____ is a tax levied on the financial income of people, corporations, or other legal entities. Various _____ systems exist, with varying degrees of tax incidence. Income taxation can be progressive, proportional, or regressive.

a. AD-IA Model
b. Income tax
c. ACCRA Cost of Living Index
d. ACEA agreement

Chapter 3. The United States

42. _____ is a field of economics concerned with paying for collective or governmental activities, and with the administration and design of those activities. The field is often divided into questions of what the government or collective organizations should do or are doing, and questions of how to pay for those activities. The broader term (public economics) and the narrower term (government finance) are also often used.
    a. Value capture
    b. Public finance
    c. Tax increment financing
    d. Minimum Municipal Obligation

43. A _____ is a consumption tax charged at the point of purchase for certain goods and services. The tax is usually set as a percentage by the government charging the tax. There is usually a list of exemptions.
    a. 130-30 fund
    b. 100-year flood
    c. Sales tax
    d. 1921 recession

44. To _____ is to impose a financial charge or other levy upon a taxpayer by a state or the functional equivalent of a state.

    _____es are also imposed by many subnational entities. _____es consist of direct _____ or indirect _____, and may be paid in money or as its labour equivalent (often but not always unpaid.)

    a. 100-year flood
    b. Tax
    c. 1921 recession
    d. 130-30 fund

45. To tax is to impose a financial charge or other levy upon a taxpayer by a state or the functional equivalent of a state.

    _____ are also imposed by many subnational entities. _____ consist of direct tax or indirect tax, and may be paid in money or as its labour equivalent (often but not always unpaid.)

    a. 130-30 fund
    b. 100-year flood
    c. 1921 recession
    d. Taxes

46. The _____ or gross domestic income (GDI), a basic measure of an economy's economic performance, is the market value of all final goods and services produced within the borders of a nation in a year. _____ can be defined in three ways, all of which are conceptually identical. First, it is equal to the total expenditures for all final goods and services produced within the country in a stipulated period of time (usually a 365-day year.)
    a. Monopolistic competition
    b. Market structure
    c. Countercyclical
    d. Gross domestic product

47. The _____ is an international financial institution that provides financial and technical assistance to developing countries for development programs (e.g. bridges, roads, schools, etc.) with the stated goal of reducing poverty.

    The _____ differs from the _____ Group, in that the _____ comprises only two institutions:

    - International Bank for Reconstruction and Development (IBRD)
    - International Development Association (IDA)

Whereas the latter incorporates these two in addition to three more:

- International Finance Corporation (IFC)
- Multilateral Investment Guarantee Agency (MIGA)
- International Centre for Settlement of Investment Disputes (ICSID)

John Maynard Keynes (right) represented the UK at the conference, and Harry Dexter White represented the US.

The _____ is one of two major financial institutions created as a result of the Bretton Woods Conference in 1944. The International Monetary Fund, a related but separate institution, is the second.

a. Bank-State-Branch
b. Flow to Equity-Approach
c. Financial costs of the 2003 Iraq War
d. World Bank

48. _____ is a dystopian novel by George Orwell. Published in England on 17 August 1945, the book reflects events leading up to and during the Stalin era before World War II. Orwell, a democratic socialist and a member of the Independent Labour Party for many years, was a critic of Joseph Stalin and was suspicious of Moscow-directed Stalinism after his experiences with the NKVD during the Spanish Civil War.

a. Adolf Hitler
b. Animal Farm
c. Adam Smith
d. Adolph Fischer

49.

_____ was the last General Secretary of the Communist Party of the Soviet Union, serving from 1985 until 1991, and also the last head of state of the USSR, serving from 1988 until its collapse in 1991. He was the only Soviet leader to have been born after the October Revolution of 1917.

Gorbachev was born in Stavropol Krai into a peasant family, and operated combine harvesters on collective farms.

a. Adolph Fischer
b. Adam Smith
c. Mikhail Sergeyevich Gorbachev
d. Adolf Hitler

Chapter 3. The United States

50. Competition law, known in the United States as _____ law, has three main elements:

- prohibiting agreements or practices that restrict free trading and competition between business entities. This includes in particular the repression of cartels.
- banning abusive behaviour by a firm dominating a market, or anti-competitive practices that tend to lead to such a dominant position. Practices controlled in this way may include predatory pricing, tying, price gouging, refusal to deal, and many others.
- supervising the mergers and acquisitions of large corporations, including some joint ventures. Transactions that are considered to threaten the competitive process can be prohibited altogether, or approved subject to 'remedies' such as an obligation to divest part of the merged business or to offer licences or access to facilities to enable other businesses to continue competing.

The substance and practice of competition law varies from jurisdiction to jurisdiction. Protecting the interests of consumers (consumer welfare) and ensuring that entrepreneurs have an opportunity to compete in the market economy are often treated as important objectives. Competition law is closely connected with law on deregulation of access to markets, state aids and subsidies, the privatisation of state owned assets and the establishment of independent sector regulators. In recent decades, competition law has been viewed as a way to provide better public services.

a. Intellectual property law
b. Antitrust
c. Anti-Inflation Act
d. United Kingdom competition law

51. The _____ is an economic and political union of 27 member states, located primarily in Europe. It was established by the Treaty of Maastricht on 1 November 1993, upon the foundations of the pre-existing European Economic Community. With a population of almost 500 million, the _____ generates an estimated 30% share (US$18.4 trillion in 2008) of the nominal gross world product.

a. ACCRA Cost of Living Index
b. European Court of Justice
c. ACEA agreement
d. European Union

52. The _____ is a federally owned corporation in the United States created by congressional charter in May 1933 to provide navigation, flood control, electricity generation, fertilizer manufacturing, and economic development in the Tennessee Valley, a region particularly impacted by the Great Depression. The _____ was envisioned not only as an electricity provider, but also as a regional economic development agency that would use federal experts and electricity to rapidly modernize the region's economy and society.

The _____'s jurisdiction covers most of Tennessee, parts of Alabama, Mississippi, and Kentucky, and small slices of Georgia, North Carolina, and Virginia.

a. 130-30 fund
b. 1921 recession
c. 100-year flood
d. Tennessee Valley Authority

53. _____ is a socioeconomic structure and political ideology that promotes the establishment of an egalitarian, classless, stateless society based on common ownership and control of the means of production and property in general. In political science, the term '_____' is sometimes used to refer to communist states, a form of government in which the state operates under a one-party system and declares allegiance to Marxism-Leninism or a derivative thereof, even if the party does not actually claim that it has already reached _____.

Forerunners of communist ideas existed in antiquity and particularly in the 18th and early 19th century France, with thinkers such as Jean-Jacques Rousseau and the more radical Gracchus Babeuf.

a. Social fascism
b. New Communist Movement
c. Communism
d. Democratic centralism

54. An _____ is a statistic about the economy. _____s allow analysis of economic performance and predictions of future performance.

_____s include various indices, earnings reports, and economic summaries, such as unemployment, housing starts, Consumer Price Index (a measure for inflation), industrial production, bankruptcies, Gross Domestic Product, broadband internet penetration, retail sales, stock market prices, and money supply changes.

a. Economic Vulnerability Index
b. Internationalization Index
c. Economic indicator
d. ACCRA Cost of Living Index

55. _____ are usually numerical time-series, i.e., sets of data (covering periods of time) for part or all of a single economy or the international economy. When they are time-series the data sets are usually monthly but can be quarterly and annual. The data may be adjusted in various ways (for ease of further analysis), most commonly adjusted or unadjusted for seasonal fluctuations.

a. ACCRA Cost of Living Index
b. ACEA agreement
c. AD-IA Model
d. Economic data

56. In mathematics, an _____ is a statement about the relative size or order of two objects, or about whether they are the same or not

- The notation a < b means that a is less than b.
- The notation a > b means that a is greater than b.
- The notation a ≠ b means that a is not equal to b, but does not say that one is greater than the other or even that they can be compared in size.

In each statement above, a is not equal to b. These relations are known as strict inequalities. The notation a < b may also be read as 'a is strictly less than b'.

a. AD-IA Model
b. ACEA agreement
c. Inequality
d. ACCRA Cost of Living Index

57. The _____ is a measure of statistical dispersion, commonly used as a measure of inequality of income distribution or inequality of wealth distribution. It is defined as a ratio with values between 0 and 1: A low _____ indicates more equal income or wealth distribution, while a high _____ indicates more unequal distribution. 0 corresponds to perfect equality (everyone having exactly the same income) and 1 corresponds to perfect inequality (where one person has all the income, while everyone else has zero income.)

a. Gini coefficient
b. Suits index
c. Compensating variation
d. Leapfrogging

58. Marxist philosophy or _____ are terms which cover work in philosophy which is strongly influenced by Karl Marx's materialist approach to theory or which is written by Marxists. It may be broadly divided into Western Marxism, which drew out of various sources, and the official philosophy in the Soviet Union, which enforced a rigid reading of Marx called 'diamat' (for 'dialectical materialism'), in particular during the 1930s. The phrase 'Marxist philosophy' itself does not indicate a strictly defined sub-field of philosophy, because the diverse influence of _____ has extended into fields as diverse as aesthetics, ethics, ontology, epistemology, and philosophy of science, as well as its obvious influence on political philosophy and the philosophy of history.
   a. 130-30 fund
   b. 1921 recession
   c. 100-year flood
   d. Marxist theory

59. The _____ of 1990 (ADA) is the short title of United States (Pub.L. 101-336, 104 Stat. 327, enacted July 26, 1990), codified at 42 U.S.C.
   a. Employment discrimination law in the United Kingdom
   b. International commercial law
   c. Expedited Funds Availability Act
   d. Americans with Disabilities Act

Chapter 4. Japan

1. A _____ describes one of a number of pieces of legislation relating to the reduction of smog and air pollution in general. The use by governments to enforce clean air standards has contributed to an improvement in human health and longer life spans. Critics argue it has also sapped corporate profits and contributed to outsourcing, while defenders counter that improved environmental air quality has generated more jobs than it has eliminated.
    a. 100-year flood
    b. 130-30 fund
    c. Smog
    d. Clean Air Act

2. The _____ is a United States federal law that requires the Environmental Protection Agency (EPA) to develop and enforce regulations to protect the general public from exposure to airborne contaminants that are known to be hazardous to human health. This law is an amendment to the Clean Air Act (CAA) originally passed in 1963.
    a. Competition law
    b. Beneficial ownership
    c. Clean Air Act Extension of 1970
    d. Meat Inspection Act

3. The _____ , or Meiji era, denotes the 45-year reign of the Meiji Emperor, running, in the Gregorian calendar, from 23 October 1868 to 30 July 1912. During this time, Japan started its modernization and rose to world power status. This era name means 'Enlightened Rule'.
    a. 100-year flood
    b. 130-30 fund
    c. 1921 recession
    d. Meiji period

4. _____ is the shortage of common things such as food, clothing, shelter and safe drinking water, all of which determine the quality of life. It may also include the lack of access to opportunities such as education and employment which aid the escape from _____ and/or allow one to enjoy the respect of fellow citizens. According to Mollie Orshansky who developed the _____ measurements used by the U.S. government, 'to be poor is to be deprived of those goods and services and pleasures which others around us take for granted.' Ongoing debates over causes, effects and best ways to measure _____, directly influence the design and implementation of _____-reduction programs and are therefore relevant to the fields of public administration and international development.
    a. Liberal welfare reforms
    b. Growth Elasticity of Poverty
    c. Poverty map
    d. Poverty

5. The _____, published in 1998 (with an epilogue added to the 1999 paperback edition), is a book by David Landes, currently Emeritus Professor of Economics and former Coolidge Professor of History at Harvard University. In it, Landes explains the 'European Miracle', or why European societies experienced a period of explosive growth when the rest of the world did not.

In doing so, he revives, at least in part, several theories he believes have been unfairly discarded by academics over the last 40 years.

    a. Human Action
    b. Wealth and Poverty of Nations
    c. The General Theory of Employment, Interest and Money
    d. Banks and Politics in America

6. A _____ is a set of companies with interlocking business relationships and shareholdings. It is a type of business group.

The prototypical _____ are those which appeared in Japan during the 'economic miracle' following World War II.

Chapter 4. Japan

a. 100-year flood
b. 1921 recession
c. 130-30 fund
d. Keiretsu

7. _____s is the social science that studies the production, distribution, and consumption of goods and services. The term _____s comes from the Ancient Greek οἰκονομῐ́α from οἶκος (oikos, 'house') + νόμος (nomos, 'custom' or 'law'), hence 'rules of the house(hold)'. Current _____ models developed out of the broader field of political economy in the late 19th century, owing to a desire to use an empirical approach more akin to the physical sciences.

a. Inflation
b. Energy economics
c. Economic
d. Opportunity cost

8. _____ are usually numerical time-series, i.e., sets of data (covering periods of time) for part or all of a single economy or the international economy. When they are time-series the data sets are usually monthly but can be quarterly and annual. The data may be adjusted in various ways (for ease of further analysis), most commonly adjusted or unadjusted for seasonal fluctuations.

a. ACEA agreement
b. ACCRA Cost of Living Index
c. AD-IA Model
d. Economic data

9. _____ is a dystopian novel by George Orwell. Published in England on 17 August 1945, the book reflects events leading up to and during the Stalin era before World War II. Orwell, a democratic socialist and a member of the Independent Labour Party for many years, was a critic of Joseph Stalin and was suspicious of Moscow-directed Stalinism after his experiences with the NKVD during the Spanish Civil War.

a. Adolph Fischer
b. Adolf Hitler
c. Adam Smith
d. Animal Farm

10. _____ Group is one of the largest corporate conglomerates (Keiretsu) in Japan and one of the largest publicly traded companies in the world. Surugacho (Suruga Street) (1856), from One Hundred Famous Views of Edo, by Hiroshige, depicting the Echigoya kimono and money exchange store with Mount Fuji in background. Currently, the _____ Main Building (ä¸‰äº•æœ¬é¤¨), which houses Sumitomo _____ Banking Corporation, _____ Fudosan, The Chuo _____ Trust and Banking Co.

a. 130-30 fund
b. 100-year flood
c. 1921 recession
d. Mitsui

11. Competition law, known in the United States as _____ law, has three main elements:

- prohibiting agreements or practices that restrict free trading and competition between business entities. This includes in particular the repression of cartels.
- banning abusive behaviour by a firm dominating a market, or anti-competitive practices that tend to lead to such a dominant position. Practices controlled in this way may include predatory pricing, tying, price gouging, refusal to deal, and many others.
- supervising the mergers and acquisitions of large corporations, including some joint ventures. Transactions that are considered to threaten the competitive process can be prohibited altogether, or approved subject to 'remedies' such as an obligation to divest part of the merged business or to offer licences or access to facilities to enable other businesses to continue competing.

The substance and practice of competition law varies from jurisdiction to jurisdiction. Protecting the interests of consumers (consumer welfare) and ensuring that entrepreneurs have an opportunity to compete in the market economy are often treated as important objectives. Competition law is closely connected with law on deregulation of access to markets, state aids and subsidies, the privatisation of state owned assets and the establishment of independent sector regulators. In recent decades, competition law has been viewed as a way to provide better public services.

a. Anti-Inflation Act
b. Intellectual property law
c. Antitrust
d. United Kingdom competition law

12. In economics, an _____ is any good or commodity, transported from one country to another country in a legitimate fashion, typically for use in trade. _____ goods or services are provided to foreign consumers by domestic producers. _____ is an important part of international trade.

a. ACCRA Cost of Living Index
b. ACEA agreement
c. AD-IA Model
d. Export

13. _____ is a Japanese term referring to industrial and financial business conglomerates in the Empire of Japan, whose influence and size allowed for control over significant parts of the Japanese economy from the Meiji period until the end of the Pacific War. Marunouchi Headquarters for Mitsubishi _____, pre-1923

Although _____ existed from the 19th century, the term was not in common use until after World War I. By definition, the '_____' were large family-controlled vertical monopolies consisting of a holding company on top, with a wholly-owned banking subsidiary providing finance, and several industrial subsidiaries dominating specific sectors of a market, either solely, or through a number of sub-subsidiary companies.

The _____ were the heart of economic and industrial activity within the Empire of Japan, and held great influence over Japanese national and foreign policies.

a. 130-30 fund
b. 100-year flood
c. 1921 recession
d. Zaibatsu

14. _____ is a name for an ideal community or society, taken from the title of a book written in 1516 by Sir Thomas More describing a fictional island in the Atlantic Ocean, possessing a seemingly perfect socio-politico-legal system. The term has been used to describe both intentional communities that attempted to create an ideal society, and fictional societies portrayed in literature. '_____' is sometimes used pejoratively, in reference to an unrealistic ideal that is impossible to achieve, and has spawned other concepts, most prominently dystopia.

a. ACEA agreement
b. ACCRA Cost of Living Index
c. AD-IA Model
d. Utopia

15. The _____ is the part of economic and administrative life that deals with the delivery of goods and services by and for the government, whether national, regional or local/municipal.

Examples of _____ activity range from delivering social security, administering urban planning and organising national defenses.

The organization of the _____ can take several forms, including:

- Direct administration funded through taxation; the delivering organization generally has no specific requirement to meet commercial success criteria, and production decisions are determined by government.
- Publicly owned corporations (in some contexts, especially manufacturing, 'state-owned enterprises'); which differ from direct administration in that they have greater commercial freedoms and are expected to operate according to commercial criteria, and production decisions are not generally taken by government (although goals may be set for them by government.)
- Partial outsourcing (of the scale many businesses do, e.g. for IT services), is considered a _____ model.

A borderline form is

- Complete outsourcing or contracting out, with a privately owned corporation delivering the entire service on behalf of government. This may be considered a mixture of private sector operations with public ownership of assets, although in some forms the private sector's control and/or risk is so great that the service may no longer be considered part of the _____.

a. Policy cycle
c. Public sector
b. 130-30 fund
d. 100-year flood

16. The _____ was an early English joint-stock company that was formed initially for pursuing trade with the East Indies, but that ended up trading with the Indian subcontinent and China. The oldest among several similarly formed European East India Companies, the Company was granted an English Royal Charter, under the name Governor and Company of Merchants of London Trading into the East Indies, by Elizabeth I on 31 December 1600. After a rival English company challenged its monopoly in the late 17th century, the two companies were merged in 1708 to form the United Company of Merchants of England Trading to the East Indies, commonly styled the Honourable _____, and abbreviated, HEast India Company; the Company was colloquially referred to as John Company, and in India as Company Bahadur.

a. ACCRA Cost of Living Index
c. East India Company
b. ACEA agreement
d. AD-IA Model

17. _____ is exchange of capital, goods, and services across international borders or territories. In most countries, it represents a significant share of gross domestic product (GDP.) While _____ has been present throughout much of history, its economic, social, and political importance has been on the rise in recent centuries.

a. Intra-industry trade
c. Import license
b. International Trade
d. Incoterms

18. The _____ is a cabinet position in a government.

A minister of finance (also called financial affairs, the treasury, the economy, or economic affairs) has many different jobs in a government. He or she helps form the government budget, stimulate the economy, and control finances.

a. 1921 recession
c. 130-30 fund
b. 100-year flood
d. Finance minister

19. The _____ was one of the most powerful agencies in the Japanese government. At the height of its influence, it effectively ran much of Japanese industrial policy, funding research and directing investment. In 2001, its role was taken over by the newly created Ministry of Economy, Trade, and Industry (METI.)
   a. 100-year flood
   b. 1921 recession
   c. Ministry of International Trade and Industry
   d. 130-30 fund

20. The _____ of the United States (Ex-Im Bank) is the official export credit agency of the United States federal government. It was established in 1934 by an executive order, and made an independent agency in the Executive branch by Congress in 1945, for the purposes of financing and insuring foreign purchases of United States goods for customers unable or unwilling to accept credit risk. The mission of the Bank is to create and sustain U.S. jobs by financing sales of U.S. exports to international buyers.
   a. Export-Import Bank
   b. AD-IA Model
   c. ACCRA Cost of Living Index
   d. ACEA agreement

21. The _____ consists of a number of economic theories which describe the nature of the firm, company including its existence, its behaviour, and its relationship with the market.

In simplified terms, the _____ aims to answer these questions:

   1. Existence - why do firms emerge, why are not all transactions in the economy mediated over the market?
   2. Boundaries - why the boundary between firms and the market is located exactly there? Which transactions are performed internally and which are negotiated on the market?
   3. Organization - why are firms structured in such specific way? What is the interplay of formal and informal relationships?

Despite looking simple, these questions are not answered by the established economic theory, which usually views firms as given, and treats them as black boxes without any internal structure.

The First World War period saw a change of emphasis in economic theory away from industry-level analysis which mainly included analysing markets to analysis at the level of the firm, as it became increasingly clear that perfect competition was no longer an adequate model of how firms behaved. Economic theory till then had focussed on trying to understand markets alone and there had been little study on understanding why firms or organisations exist.

   a. Policy Ineffectiveness Proposition
   b. Khazzoom-Brookes postulate
   c. Technology gap
   d. Theory of the firm

22. A _____ is a business that is privately owned and operated, with a small number of employees and relatively low volume of sales. The legal definition of 'small' often varies by country and industry, but is generally under 100 employees in the United States and under 50 employees in the European Union. In comparison, the definition of mid-sized business by the number of employees is generally under 500 in the U.S. and 250 for the European Union.

a. Procurement
b. Small Business
c. Cabotage
d. Farmshoring

23. _____ is the process by which the government, central bank (ii) availability of money, and (iii) cost of money or rate of interest, in order to attain a set of objectives oriented towards the growth and stability of the economy. Monetary theory provides insight into how to craft optimal _____.

_____ is referred to as either being an expansionary policy where an expansionary policy increases the total supply of money in the economy, and a contractionary policy decreases the total money supply.

a. 130-30 fund
b. Monetary policy
c. 100-year flood
d. 1921 recession

24. A _____ or labor union is an organization of workers who have banded together to achieve common goals in key areas and working conditions. The _____, through its leadership, bargains with the employer on behalf of union members (rank and file members) and negotiates labor contracts (Collective bargaining) with employers. This may include the negotiation of wages, work rules, complaint procedures, rules governing hiring, firing and promotion of workers, benefits, workplace safety and policies.

a. Guaranteed investment contracts
b. Case-Shiller Home Price Indices
c. Consumer goods
d. Trade union

25. General _____ was a Nigerian military leader and politician. He was the de facto President of Nigeria from 1993 to 1998.

Abacha was a Muslim of Kanuri extraction.

a. Sani Abacha
b. Sir Harold Matthew Evans
c. Peter Ferdinand Drucker
d. Thomas Mun

26. _____ was a survey conducted by the U.S. Department of Justice to gauge the prevalence of alcohol and illegal drug use among prior arrestees. It was a reformulation of the prior Drug Use Forecasting (DUF) program, focused on five drugs in particular: cocaine, marijuana, methamphetamine, opiates, and PCP.

Participants were randomly selected from arrest records in major metropolitan areas; because no personally identifying information is taken from each record chosen, the resulting data can be correlated to arrest rates, but not to the total population of persons charged.

a. AD-IA Model
b. ACCRA Cost of Living Index
c. ACEA agreement
d. Arrestee Drug Abuse Monitoring

27. A political party described as a _____ includes those that advocate the application of the social principles of communism through a communist form of government. The name originates from the 1848 tract Manifesto of the _____ by Karl Marx, Friedrich Engels. The Leninist concept of a _____ encompases a larger political system and includes not only an ideological orientation but also a wide set of organizational policies.

a. Communist Party
b. Criticisms of Communist party rule
c. Criticisms of anarcho-capitalism
d. Communism

28. _____ was a Swedish economist and politician. He was a professor of economics at the Stockholm School of Economics from 1929 to 1965. He was also leader of the People's Party, a social-liberal party which at the time was the largest party in opposition to the governing Social Democratic Party, from 1944 to 1967.
   a. Nicholas II
   b. Maximilian Carl Emil Weber
   c. Martin Luther
   d. Bertil Gotthard Ohlin

29. _____ was a Scottish moral philosopher and a pioneer of political economy. One of the key figures of the Scottish Enlightenment, Smith is the author of The Theory of Moral Sentiments and An Inquiry into the Nature and Causes of the Wealth of Nations. The latter, usually abbreviated as The Wealth of Nations, is considered his magnum opus and the first modern work of economics.
   a. Alan Greenspan
   b. Adolph Fischer
   c. Adolf Hitler
   d. Adam Smith

30. In economics, _____ refers to the ability of a party to produce a good or service using fewer real resources than another entity producing the same good or service..A party has an _____ when using the same input as another party, it can produce a greater output. Since _____ is determined by a simple comparison of labor productivities, it is possible for a a party to have no _____ in anything. It can be contrasted with the concept of comparative advantage which refers to the ability to produce a particular good at a lower opportunity cost.
   a. International economics
   b. ACCRA Cost of Living Index
   c. Absolute advantage
   d. Index number

31. In economics, _____ refers to the ability of a person or a country to produce a particular good at a lower marginal cost and opportunity cost than another person or country. It is the ability to produce a product most efficiently given all the other products that could be produced. It can be contrasted with absolute advantage which refers to the ability of a person or a country to produce a particular good at a lower absolute cost than another.
   a. Triffin dilemma
   b. Comparative advantage
   c. Hot money
   d. Gravity model of trade

32. In economics a country's _____ is commonly understood as the amount of land, labor, capital, and entrepreneurship that a country possesses and can exploit for manufacturing. Countries with a large endowment of resources tend to be more prosperous than those with a small endowment, all other things being equal. The development of sound institutions to access and equitably distribute these resources, however, is necessary in order for a country to obtain the greatest benefit from its _____.
   a. Factor endowment
   b. Dutch disease
   c. Foreign Affiliate Trade Statistics
   d. Price scissors

33. The _____ , 1949-1991, was an economic organization of communist states and a kind of Eastern Bloc equivalent to--but more geographically inclusive than--the European Economic Community. The military equivalent to the Comecon was the Warsaw Pact, though Comecon's membership was significantly wider. The Comecon was the Eastern Bloc's reply to the formation of the OEEC .
   a. 100-year flood
   b. 130-30 fund
   c. 1921 recession
   d. Council for Mutual Economic Assistance

34. In finance, _____ is investment originating from other countries. See Foreign direct investment.
   a. Horizontal merger
   b. Foreign investment
   c. Demand side economics
   d. Preclusive purchasing

Chapter 5. Germany

1. _____ was a survey conducted by the U.S. Department of Justice to gauge the prevalence of alcohol and illegal drug use among prior arrestees. It was a reformulation of the prior Drug Use Forecasting (DUF) program, focused on five drugs in particular: cocaine, marijuana, methamphetamine, opiates, and PCP.

Participants were randomly selected from arrest records in major metropolitan areas; because no personally identifying information is taken from each record chosen, the resulting data can be correlated to arrest rates, but not to the total population of persons charged.

   a. ACEA agreement
   b. ACCRA Cost of Living Index
   c. AD-IA Model
   d. Arrestee Drug Abuse Monitoring

2. _____ was a Scottish moral philosopher and a pioneer of political economy. One of the key figures of the Scottish Enlightenment, Smith is the author of The Theory of Moral Sentiments and An Inquiry into the Nature and Causes of the Wealth of Nations. The latter, usually abbreviated as The Wealth of Nations, is considered his magnum opus and the first modern work of economics.
   a. Alan Greenspan
   b. Adolf Hitler
   c. Adolph Fischer
   d. Adam Smith

3. _____ was a German economist and sociologist, the head of the 'Youngest Historical School' and one of the leading Continental European social scientists during the first quarter of the 20th century.

He was born in Ermsleben, Harz, as the son of a wealthy liberal politician, industrialist, and estate-owner, Anton Ludwig Sombart, and studied at the universities of Pisa, Berlin, and Rome, both law and economics. In 1888, he received his Ph.D. from Berlin under the direction of Gustav von Schmoller and Adolph Wagner, then the most eminent German economists.

   a. Martin Luther
   b. Thomas Mun
   c. George Cabot Lodge II
   d. Werner Sombart

4. _____ was a German lawyer, politician, scholar, political economist and sociologist, who profoundly influenced sociological theory.

Weber's major works deal with rationalization in sociology of religion, government, organizational theory, and behavior. His most famous work is his essay The Protestant Ethic and the Spirit of Capitalism, which began his work in the sociology of religion.

   a. Peter Ferdinand Drucker
   b. Martin Luther
   c. George Cabot Lodge II
   d. Maximilian Carl Emil Weber

5. The _____ was a physical barrier completely encircling West Berlin, separating it from the German Democratic Republic, including East Berlin. The longer inner German border demarcated the border between East and West Germany. Both borders came to symbolize the Iron Curtain between Western Europe and the Eastern Bloc.
   a. Berlin Wall
   b. Cold War
   c. Sino-Soviet split
   d. Reagan Doctrine

Chapter 5. Germany

6. _____s is the social science that studies the production, distribution, and consumption of goods and services. The term _____s comes from the Ancient Greek oá¼°κονομῖα from oá¼¶κος (oikos, 'house') + vÏŒμος (nomos, 'custom' or 'law'), hence 'rules of the house(hold)'. Current _____ models developed out of the broader field of political economy in the late 19th century, owing to a desire to use an empirical approach more akin to the physical sciences.

a. Economic
b. Inflation
c. Opportunity cost
d. Energy economics

7. The _____, German Deutsches Institut für Wirtschaftsforschung is one of the leading economic research institutes in Germany. It is an independent, non-profit academic institution which is involved in basic research and policy advice. DIW Berlin was originally founded in 1925 as Institute for Business Cycle Research and was later renamed to its current name.

a. 1921 recession
b. German Institute for Economic Research
c. 100-year flood
d. 130-30 fund

8. _____ normally means a German [/Austrian /Swiss] small and medium-sized enterprise . Economic and business historians have to an increasing degree been giving _____ companies more and more the credit for Germany's economic growth in the beginning of the 20th century.

Exactly defining _____ companies is difficult, because the word (directly translated) refers to 'middle class'.

a. Congress of Industrial Organizations
b. Mittelstand
c. Non-governmental organization
d. Dogwood Alliance

9. The _____ was a self-declared socialist state (but often referred to in the West as a 'communist state') in the Eastern Bloc created in the Soviet Zone of occupied Germany and the Soviet sector of occupied Berlin. The _____ existed from 7 October 1949 until 3 October 1990, when its re-established states acceded to the adjacent Federal Republic of Germany, thus producing the current form of the state of Germany.

In 1955, the Soviet Union declared that the Republic was fully sovereign.

a. Adolf Hitler
b. Adam Smith
c. Adolph Fischer
d. German Democratic Republic

10. _____ was the common English name for the Federal Republic of Germany , from its formation in May 1949 to German reunification in October 1990, when East Germany was dissolved and its states became part of the Federal Republic, ending the more than 40-year division of Germany. From the 1990 reunification onwards, the Federal Republic of Germany has been commonly known as Germany.

The Federal Republic of Germany was formed from the three Western Zones or Allied Zones of occupation held by the United States, the United Kingdom, and France.

a. 1921 recession
b. 130-30 fund
c. West Germany
d. 100-year flood

11. An economic and _____ is a single market with a common currency. It is to be distinguished from a mere currency union , which does not involve a single market. This is the fifth stage of economic integration.

a. Free trade zone
b. Customs union
c. Commercial invoice
d. Monetary union

12. In economics _____ is defined as the sum of private and external costs. Economic theorists ascribe individual decision-making to a calculation costs and benefits. Rational choice theory assumes that individuals only consider their own private costs when making decisions, not the costs that may be borne by others.

a. Cost-Volume-Profit Analysis
b. Khozraschyot
c. Psychic cost
d. Social cost

13. The Great Proletarian _____ in the People's Republic of China was a period of widespread social and political upheaval; the nation-wide chaos and economic disarray engulfed much of Chinese society between 1966 and 1976.

It was launched by Mao Zedong, the chairman of the Communist Party of China, on May 16, 1966, who alleged that liberal bourgeoisie elements were dominating the party and insisted that they needed to be removed through post-revolutionary class struggle by mobilizing the thoughts and actions of China's youth, who formed Red Guards groups around the country. Although Mao himself officially declared the _____ to have ended in 1969, today it is widely believed that the power struggles and political instability between 1969 and the arrest of the Gang of Four as well as the death of Mao in 1976 were also part of the Revolution.

a. 130-30 fund
b. 100-year flood
c. 1921 recession
d. Cultural Revolution

14. A _____ is the exclusive authority to determine how a resource is used, whether that resource is owned by government or by individuals. All economic goods have a _____s attribute. This attribute has three broad components

1. The right to use the good
2. The right to earn income from the good
3. The right to transfer the good to others

The concept of _____s as used by economists and legal scholars are related but distinct. The distinction is largely seen in the economists' focus on the ability of an individual or collective to control the use of the good.

a. Holder in due course
b. Post-sale restraint
c. High-reeve
d. Property right

15. _____ is sometimes referred to as _____, actually it means Economic Monetary Union.

First ideas of an economic and monetary union in Europe were raised well before establishing the European Communities. For example, already in the League of Nations, Gustav Stresemann asked in 1929 for a European currency (Link) against the background of an increased economic division due to a number of new nation states in Europe after WWI.

a. Euro Interbank Offered Rate
b. European Monetary Union
c. Exchange rate mechanism
d. European Monetary System

Chapter 5. Germany

16. _____ are usually numerical time-series, i.e., sets of data (covering periods of time) for part or all of a single economy or the international economy. When they are time-series the data sets are usually monthly but can be quarterly and annual. The data may be adjusted in various ways (for ease of further analysis), most commonly adjusted or unadjusted for seasonal fluctuations.
    a. AD-IA Model
    b. Economic data
    c. ACEA agreement
    d. ACCRA Cost of Living Index

17. A _____, reserve bank, or monetary authority is the entity responsible for the monetary policy of a country or of a group of member states. It is a bank that can lend money to other banks in times of need. Its primary responsibility is to maintain the stability of the national currency and money supply, but more active duties include controlling subsidized-loan interest rates, and acting as a lender of last resort to the banking sector during times of financial crisis (private banks often being integral to the national financial system.)
    a. 1921 recession
    b. 100-year flood
    c. 130-30 fund
    d. Central Bank

18. The _____ is the central bank of the Federal Republic of Germany and as such part of the European System of Central Banks. Due to its strength and former size, the Bundesbank is the most influential member of the ESCB. Both the _____ and the European Central Bank (ECB) are located in Frankfurt am Main.
    a. 100-year flood
    b. 130-30 fund
    c. 1921 recession
    d. Deutsche Bundesbank

19. The _____ is an economic and political union of 27 member states, located primarily in Europe. It was established by the Treaty of Maastricht on 1 November 1993, upon the foundations of the pre-existing European Economic Community. With a population of almost 500 million, the _____ generates an estimated 30% share (US$18.4 trillion in 2008) of the nominal gross world product.
    a. ACCRA Cost of Living Index
    b. ACEA agreement
    c. European Court of Justice
    d. European Union

20. _____ changed the course of Western civilization by initiating the Protestant Reformation. As a priest and theology professor, he confronted indulgence salesmen with his 95 Theses in 1517. Luther strongly disputed their claim that freedom from God's punishment of sin could be purchased with money.
    a. Henry Ford
    b. George Cabot Lodge II
    c. Maximilian Carl Emil Weber
    d. Martin Luther

21. The _____, sometimes called the Puritan Work Ethic, is a sociological, theoretical concept. It is based upon the notion that the Calvinist emphasis on the necessity for hard work is proponent of a person's calling and worldly success is a sign of personal salvation. It is argued that Protestants beginning with Martin Luther had reconceptualised worldly work as a duty which benefits both the individual and society as a whole.
    a. 100-year flood
    b. 130-30 fund
    c. Protestant work ethic
    d. 1921 recession

22. _____ AG is an international Universal bank with its headquarters in Frankfurt, Germany. The bank employs more than 81,000 people in 76 countries, and has a large presence in Europe, the Americas, Asia Pacific and the emerging markets.

_____ has offices in major financial centers, such as London, Moscow, New York, São Paulo, Singapore, Sydney, Hong Kong and Tokyo.

a. Paris Club
b. Federal Deposit Insurance Corporation
c. Chinese correction
d. Deutsche Bank

23. Co-determination is a practice whereby the employees have a role in management of a company. The word is a somewhat clumsy and literal translation from the German word Mitbestimmung. _____ rights are different in different legal environments.

a. Formula for Change
b. Codetermination
c. Span of control
d. Business plan

24. A _____ or labor union is an organization of workers who have banded together to achieve common goals in key areas and working conditions. The _____, through its leadership, bargains with the employer on behalf of union members (rank and file members) and negotiates labor contracts (Collective bargaining) with employers. This may include the negotiation of wages, work rules, complaint procedures, rules governing hiring, firing and promotion of workers, benefits, workplace safety and policies.

a. Trade union
b. Guaranteed investment contracts
c. Consumer goods
d. Case-Shiller Home Price Indices

25. _____, in law and economics, is a form of risk management primarily used to hedge against the risk of a contingent loss. _____ is defined as the equitable transfer of the risk of a loss, from one entity to another, in exchange for a premium, and can be thought of as a guaranteed small loss to prevent a large, possibly devastating loss. An insurer is a company selling the _____; an insured or policyholder is the person or entity buying the _____.

a. ACEA agreement
b. AD-IA Model
c. ACCRA Cost of Living Index
d. Insurance

26. Wisconsin originated the idea of _____ in the U.S. in 1932. In the United States, there are 50 state _____ programs plus one each in the District of Columbia and Puerto Rico. Through the Social Security Act of 1935, the Federal Government of the United States effectively coerced the individual states into adopting _____ plans.

a. Unemployment insurance
b. ACEA agreement
c. AD-IA Model
d. ACCRA Cost of Living Index

27. In general, a _____ is an arrangement to provide people with an income when they are no longer earning a regular income from employment.

The terms retirement plan or superannuation refer to a _____ granted upon retirement . Retirement plans may be set up by employers, insurance companies, the government or other institutions such as employer associations or trade unions.

a. Profit-sharing agreement
b. Pension
c. Superannuation
d. Real wage

Chapter 5. Germany

28. The _____ or gross domestic income (GDI), a basic measure of an economy's economic performance, is the market value of all final goods and services produced within the borders of a nation in a year. _____ can be defined in three ways, all of which are conceptually identical. First, it is equal to the total expenditures for all final goods and services produced within the country in a stipulated period of time (usually a 365-day year.)
   a. Market structure
   b. Monopolistic competition
   c. Gross domestic product
   d. Countercyclical

29. A _____ product is a product designed for cheapness and short-term convenience rather than medium to long-term durability, with most products only intended for single use. The term is also sometimes used for products that may last several months (ex. _____ air filters) to distinguish from similar products that last indefinitely (ex.
   a. Disposable
   b. 100-year flood
   c. 130-30 fund
   d. 1921 recession

30. _____ is gross income minus income tax on that income.

Discretionary income is income after subtracting taxes and normal expenses (such as rent or mortgage, utilities, insurance, medical, transportation, property maintenance, child support, inflation, food and sundries, 'c.) to maintain a certain standard of living.

   a. Taxation as theft
   b. Disposable personal income
   c. Stamp Act
   d. Disposable income

31. The _____ established the Federal Deposit Insurance Corporation (FDIC) in the United States and included banking reforms, some of which were designed to control speculation. Some provisions such as Regulation Q, which allowed the Federal Reserve to regulate interest rates in savings accounts, were repealed by the Depository Institutions Deregulation and Monetary Control Act of 1980. Provisions that prohibit a bank holding company from owning other financial companies were repealed on November 12, 1999, by the Gramm-Leach-Bliley Act.
   a. Glass-Steagall Act of 1933
   b. 100-year flood
   c. 130-30 fund
   d. 1921 recession

32. The _____ was the primary plan of the United States for rebuilding and creating a stronger foundation for the countries of Western Europe, and repelling communism after World War II. The initiative was named for Secretary of State George Marshall and was largely the creation of State Department officials, especially William L. Clayton and George F. Kennan. George Marshall spoke of the administration's want to help European recovery in his address at Harvard University in June 1947.
   a. 100-year flood
   b. 130-30 fund
   c. 1921 recession
   d. Marshall Plan

Chapter 6. Socialism as an Economic System

1. A political party described as a _____ includes those that advocate the application of the social principles of communism through a communist form of government. The name originates from the 1848 tract Manifesto of the _____ by Karl Marx, Friedrich Engels. The Leninist concept of a _____ encompasses a larger political system and includes not only an ideological orientation but also a wide set of organizational policies.
    a. Criticisms of Communist party rule
    b. Criticisms of anarcho-capitalism
    c. Communism
    d. Communist Party

2. _____ is a socioeconomic structure and political ideology that promotes the establishment of an egalitarian, classless, stateless society based on common ownership and control of the means of production and property in general. In political science, the term '_____' is sometimes used to refer to communist states, a form of government in which the state operates under a one-party system and declares allegiance to Marxism-Leninism or a derivative thereof, even if the party does not actually claim that it has already reached _____.

Forerunners of communist ideas existed in antiquity and particularly in the 18th and early 19th century France, with thinkers such as Jean-Jacques Rousseau and the more radical Gracchus Babeuf.

    a. Democratic centralism
    b. Social fascism
    c. New Communist Movement
    d. Communism

3. _____ in political thought refers to economic theories of social organization advocating collective ownership and administration of the means of production and distribution of goods, and a society characterized by equality for all individuals, with an egalitarian method of compensation. Modern _____ originated in the late 19th-century intellectual and working class political movement that criticized the effects of industrialization and private ownership on society. Karl Marx posited that _____ would be achieved via class struggle and a proletarian revolution after a transitional stage from capitalism called the dictatorship of the proletariat.
    a. Adolph Fischer
    b. Adolf Hitler
    c. Socialism
    d. Adam Smith

4. The Great Proletarian _____ in the People's Republic of China was a period of widespread social and political upheaval; the nation-wide chaos and economic disarray engulfed much of Chinese society between 1966 and 1976.

It was launched by Mao Zedong, the chairman of the Communist Party of China, on May 16, 1966, who alleged that liberal bourgeoisie elements were dominating the party and insisted that they needed to be removed through post-revolutionary class struggle by mobilizing the thoughts and actions of China's youth, who formed Red Guards groups around the country. Although Mao himself officially declared the _____ to have ended in 1969, today it is widely believed that the power struggles and political instability between 1969 and the arrest of the Gang of Four as well as the death of Mao in 1976 were also part of the Revolution.

    a. 130-30 fund
    b. 100-year flood
    c. 1921 recession
    d. Cultural Revolution

5. _____ was a German lawyer, politician, scholar, political economist and sociologist, who profoundly influenced sociological theory.

Weber's major works deal with rationalization in sociology of religion, government, organizational theory, and behavior. His most famous work is his essay The Protestant Ethic and the Spirit of Capitalism, which began his work in the sociology of religion.

Chapter 6. Socialism as an Economic System

a. Peter Ferdinand Drucker
b. Martin Luther
c. George Cabot Lodge II
d. Maximilian Carl Emil Weber

6. A _____ is the exclusive authority to determine how a resource is used, whether that resource is owned by government or by individuals. All economic goods have a _____s attribute. This attribute has three broad components

    1. The right to use the good
    2. The right to earn income from the good
    3. The right to transfer the good to others

The concept of _____s as used by economists and legal scholars are related but distinct. The distinction is largely seen in the economists' focus on the ability of an individual or collective to control the use of the good.

a. High-reeve
b. Property right
c. Post-sale restraint
d. Holder in due course

7. There are two main interpretations of the idea of a _____:

    - A model in which the state assumes primary responsibility for the welfare of its citizens. This responsibility in theory ought to be comprehensive, because all aspects of welfare are considered and universally applied to citizens as a 'right'. _____ can also mean the creation of a 'social safety net' of minimum standards of varying forms of welfare. Here is found some confusion between a '_____' and a 'welfare society' in common debate about the definition of the term.
    - The provision of welfare in society. In many '_____s', especially in continental Europe, welfare is not actually provided by the state, but by a combination of independent, voluntary, mutualist and government services. The functional provider of benefits and services may be a central or state government, a state-sponsored company or agency, a private corporation, a charity or another form of non-profit organization. However, this phenomenon has been more appropriately termed a 'welfare society,' and the term 'welfare system' has been used to describe the range of _____ and welfare society mixes that are found.

The English term '_____' is believed by Asa Briggs to have been coined by Archbishop William Temple during the Second World War, contrasting wartime Britain with the 'warfare state' of Nazi Germany. Friedrich Hayek contends that the term derived from the older German word Wohlfahrtsstaat, which itself was used by nineteenth century historians to describe a variant of the ideal of Polizeistaat . It was fully developed by the German academic Sozialpolitiker--'socialists of the chair'--from 1870 and first implemented through Bismarck's 'state socialism'. Bismarck's policies have also been seen as the creation of a _____.

a. 100-year flood
b. 130-30 fund
c. Welfare state
d. 1921 recession

8. The _____ was a period of political and social upheaval and radical change in the history of France, during which the French governmental structure, previously an absolute monarchy with feudal privileges for the aristocracy and Catholic clergy, underwent radical change to forms based on Enlightenment principles of citizenship and inalienable rights.

These changes were accompanied by violent turmoil which included the trial and execution of the king, vast bloodshed and repression during the Reign of Terror, and warfare involving every other major European power. Subsequent events that can be traced to the Revolution include the Napoleonic Wars, two separate restorations of the monarchy, and two additional revolutions as modern France took shape.

- a. 1921 recession
- b. French Revolution
- c. 100-year flood
- d. 130-30 fund

9. Sir _____ was an English lawyer, author, and statesman who in his lifetime gained a reputation as a leading Renaissance humanist scholar, and occupied many public offices, including Lord Chancellor. More coined the word 'utopia', a name he gave to the ideal, imaginary island nation whose political system he described in Utopia, published in 1516. He was beheaded in 1535 when he refused to sign the Act of Supremacy that declared King Henry VIII Supreme Head of the Church of England.

- a. Adam Smith
- b. Adolf Hitler
- c. Adolph Fischer
- d. Thomas More

10. _____ is a name for an ideal community or society, taken from the title of a book written in 1516 by Sir Thomas More describing a fictional island in the Atlantic Ocean, possessing a seemingly perfect socio-politico-legal system. The term has been used to describe both intentional communities that attempted to create an ideal society, and fictional societies portrayed in literature. '_____' is sometimes used pejoratively, in reference to an unrealistic ideal that is impossible to achieve, and has spawned other concepts, most prominently dystopia.

- a. ACEA agreement
- b. AD-IA Model
- c. ACCRA Cost of Living Index
- d. Utopia

11. _____ is a term used to define the first currents of modern socialist thought. Although it is technically possible for any person living at any time in history to be a utopian socialist, the term is most often applied to those utopian socialists who lived in the first quarter of the 19th century. From the mid-19th century onwards, the other branches of socialism overtook the utopian version in terms of intellectual development and number of supporters.

- a. AD-IA Model
- b. ACEA agreement
- c. ACCRA Cost of Living Index
- d. Utopian socialism

12. The _____ was a period in the late 18th and early 19th centuries when major changes in agriculture, manufacturing, mining, and transportation had a profound effect on the socioeconomic and cultural conditions in Britain. The changes subsequently spread throughout Europe, North America, and eventually the world. The onset of the _____ marked a major turning point in human society; almost every aspect of daily life was eventually influenced in some way.

- a. Industrial Revolution
- b. Adolph Fischer
- c. Adolf Hitler
- d. Adam Smith

13. _____, born in Newtown, Montgomeryshire, Wales was a social reformer and one of the founders of socialism and the cooperative movement.

Chapter 6. Socialism as an Economic System

Owen's philosophy was based on three intellectual pillars:

- First, no one was responsible for his will and his own actions, because his whole character is formed independently of himself; people are products of their environment, hence his support for education and labour reform, rendering him a pioneer in human capital investment.
- Second, all religions are based on the same absurd imagination, that make man a weak, imbecile animal; a furious bigot and fanatic; or a miserable hypocrite; (in dotage, he embraced Spiritualism.)
- Third, support for the putting-out system instead of the factory system.

Owen was born in Newtown, then a small market town in Montgomeryshire, Mid Wales, the sixth child of seven. His father had a small business as a saddler and ironmonger. Owen's mother came from one of the prosperous farming families; here, young Owen received almost all his school education, which terminated at the age of ten.

a. Adolph Fischer
b. Adolf Hitler
c. Adam Smith
d. Robert Owen

14. _____ in economics and business is the result of an exchange and from that trade we assign a numerical monetary value to a good, service or asset. If Alice trades Bob 4 apples for an orange, the _____ of an orange is 4 apples. Inversely, the _____ of an apple is 1/4 oranges.

a. Premium pricing
b. Price war
c. Price book
d. Price

15. A _____ or market-based mechanism is any of a wide variety of ways to match up buyers and sellers.

An example of a _____ uses announced bid and ask prices. Generally speaking, when two parties wish to engage in a trade, the purchaser will announce a price he is willing to pay (the bid price) and seller will announce a price he is willing to accept (the ask price.)

a. Market equilibrium
b. Horizontal market
c. Marketization
d. Price mechanism

16. In economics, a _____ is any economic system that effects its distribution of goods and services with prices and employing any form of money or debt tokens. Except for possible remote and primitive communities, all modern societies use _____s to allocate resources. However, _____s are not used for all resource allocation decisions today.

a. Family economy
b. Hanseatic League
c. Neomercantilism
d. Price system

17. The _____ is a regional organization whose participating countries are former Soviet Republics.

The CIS is comparable to a confederation similar to the original European Community. Although the CIS has few supranational powers, it is more than a purely symbolic organization, possessing coordinating powers in the realm of trade, finance, lawmaking, and security.

a. 130-30 fund
b. Commonwealth of Independent States
c. 1921 recession
d. 100-year flood

18. _____: Kritik der politischen Ökonomie is an extensive treatise on political economy written in German by Karl Marx and edited in part by Friedrich Engels. The book is a critical analysis of capitalism. Its first volume was published in 1867.

a. Dialectics of Nature
b. Capital accumulation
c. Das Kapital
d. Productive force

19. A _____ is an independent country whose territory consists solely of a single major city and the area immediately surrounding it. The term '_____' should not be confused with 'independent city', which refers to a city which is not administered as part of another local government.

Whereas the nation-states rely on a common cultural heritage, be it linguistic, historical, religious, economic, etc., the _____ relies on the common interest in the function of the urban center.

a. 130-30 fund
b. 1921 recession
c. 100-year flood
d. City-state

20. _____ was a survey conducted by the U.S. Department of Justice to gauge the prevalence of alcohol and illegal drug use among prior arrestees. It was a reformulation of the prior Drug Use Forecasting (DUF) program, focused on five drugs in particular: cocaine, marijuana, methamphetamine, opiates, and PCP.

Participants were randomly selected from arrest records in major metropolitan areas; because no personally identifying information is taken from each record chosen, the resulting data can be correlated to arrest rates, but not to the total population of persons charged.

a. ACCRA Cost of Living Index
b. ACEA agreement
c. AD-IA Model
d. Arrestee Drug Abuse Monitoring

21. _____, originally also Bolshevists were a faction of the Marxist Russian Social Democratic Labour Party which split apart from the Menshevik faction at the Second Party Congress in 1903 and ultimately became the Communist Party of the Soviet Union. The _____ seized power in Russia during the October Revolution phase of the Russian Revolution of 1917, and founded the Soviet Union.

_____ were an organization of professional revolutionaries under a strict internal hierarchy governed by the principle of democratic centralism and quasi-military discipline, who considered themselves as a vanguard of the revolutionary proletariat.

a. Real socialism
b. Commodity form theory
c. Redistribution game
d. Bolsheviks

Chapter 6. Socialism as an Economic System

22. Marxist philosophy or _____ are terms which cover work in philosophy which is strongly influenced by Karl Marx's materialist approach to theory or which is written by Marxists. It may be broadly divided into Western Marxism, which drew out of various sources, and the official philosophy in the Soviet Union, which enforced a rigid reading of Marx called 'diamat' (for 'dialectical materialism'), in particular during the 1930s. The phrase 'Marxist philosophy' itself does not indicate a strictly defined sub-field of philosophy, because the diverse influence of _____ has extended into fields as diverse as aesthetics, ethics, ontology, epistemology, and philosophy of science, as well as its obvious influence on political philosophy and the philosophy of history.
   - a. 100-year flood
   - b. 130-30 fund
   - c. 1921 recession
   - d. Marxist theory

23. _____ was a Scottish moral philosopher and a pioneer of political economy. One of the key figures of the Scottish Enlightenment, Smith is the author of The Theory of Moral Sentiments and An Inquiry into the Nature and Causes of the Wealth of Nations. The latter, usually abbreviated as The Wealth of Nations, is considered his magnum opus and the first modern work of economics.
   - a. Adolf Hitler
   - b. Alan Greenspan
   - c. Adolph Fischer
   - d. Adam Smith

24. _____ is a classification used in analyzing human societies to describe a social class of people. Historically, the _____ comes from the middle or merchant classes of the Middle Ages, whose status or power came from employment, education, and wealth, as distinguished from those whose power came from being born into an aristocratic family of land owners. In modern times, it is the class owning the means for producing wealth.
   - a. 130-30 fund
   - b. 100-year flood
   - c. Middle class
   - d. Bourgeoisie

25. In economics, _____ is how a natione;s total economy is distributed among its population. ._____ has always been a central concern of economic theory and economic policy. Classical economists such as Adam Smith, Thomas Malthus and David Ricardo were mainly concerned with factor _____, that is, the distribution of income between the main factors of production, land, labour and capital.
   - a. Eco commerce
   - b. Authorised capital
   - c. Income distribution
   - d. Equipment trust certificate

26. The _____ is a term used to identify a lower social class; a member of such a class is proletarian. Originally it was identified as those people who had no wealth other than their sons. The term was initially used in a derogatory sense, until Karl Marx used it as a sociological term to refer to the working class.
   - a. Faux frais of production
   - b. Differential and Absolute Ground Rent
   - c. Proletariat
   - d. Surplus value

27. _____ is a concept created by Karl Marx in his critique of political economy, where its ultimate source is unpaid surplus labor performed by the worker for the capitalist, serving as a basis for capital accumulation.

The German equivalent word 'Mehrwert' means simply value-added , but in Marx's value theory, the extra or surplus-value has a specific meaning, which is not the new value added to the output of products, but rather the amount of the increase in the value of capital upon investment, i.e. the yield or increment in value, regardless of whether it takes the form of profit, interest or rent.

Marx himself regarded the reduction of profit, interest, and rent income to surplus-value, and _____ to surplus labour as one of his greatest theoretical achievements.

a. Productive force
c. Rate of exploitation
b. Socially necessary labour time
d. Surplus value

28. _____ is the a method of technical and economic research of the systems for purpose to optimize a parity between system's consumer functions or properties and expenses to achieve those functions or properties.

This methodology for continuous perfection of production, industrial technologies, organizational structures was developed by Juryj Sobolev in 1948 at the 'Perm telephone factory'

- 1948 Juryj Sobolev - the first success in application of a method analysis at the 'Perm telephone factory' .
- 1949 - the first application for the invention as result of use of the new method.

Today in economically developed countries practically each enterprise or the company use methodology of the kind of functional-cost analysis as a practice of the quality management, most full satisfying to principles of standards of series ISO 9000.

- Interest of consumer not in products itself, but the advantage which it will receive from its usage.
- The consumer aspires to reduce his expenses
- Functions needed by consumer can be executed in the various ways, and, hence, with various efficiency and expenses. Among possible alternatives of realization of functions exist such in which the parity of quality and the price is the optimal for the consumer.

The goal of _____ is achievement of the highest consumer satisfaction of production at simultaneous decrease in all kinds of industrial expenses Classical _____ has three English synonyms - Value Engineering, Value Management, Value Analysis.

a. Willingness to pay
c. Staple financing
b. Monopoly wage
d. Function cost analysis

29. _____ is an economic system in which wealth, and the means of producing wealth, are privately owned. Through _____, the land, labor, and capital are owned, operated, and traded for the purpose of generating profits, without force or fraud, by private individuals either singly or jointly, and investments, distribution, income, production, pricing and supply of goods, commodities and services are determined by voluntary private decision in a market economy. A distinguishing feature of _____ is that each person owns his or her own labor and therefore is allowed to sell the use of it to employers.

a. Late capitalism
c. Socialism for the rich and capitalism for the poor
b. Creative capitalism
d. Capitalism

30.

_____ was a German philosopher, political economist, historian, political theorist, sociologist, communist and revolutionary credited as the founder of communism.

Chapter 6. Socialism as an Economic System 55

Marx summarized his approach to history and politics in the opening line of the first chapter of The Communist Manifesto : e;The history of all hitherto existing society is the history of class struggles.e; Marx argued that capitalism, like previous socioeconomic systems, will produce internal tensions which will lead to its destruction. Just as capitalism replaced feudalism, socialism will in its turn replace capitalism and lead to a stateless, classless society which will emerge after a transitional period, the 'dictatorship of the proletariat'.

   a. Neo-Gramscianism   b. Karl Heinrich Marx
   c. Adam Smith   d. Marxism

31. _____ refers to how a person or group chooses to spend their resources, particularly money and time. Literally, a materialist is a person for whom collecting material goods is an important priority. In common use, the word more specifically refers to a person who primarily pursues wealth and luxury.
   a. Global justice   b. Philosophy of economics
   c. Political philosophy   d. Materialism

32. _____ is a method of argument, which has been central to both Eastern and Western philosophy since ancient times. The word '_____' originates in Ancient Greece, and was made popular by Plato's Socratic dialogues. _____ is rooted in the ordinary practice of a dialogue between two people who hold different ideas and wish to persuade each other.
   a. 130-30 fund   b. Dialectic
   c. 1921 recession   d. 100-year flood

33. _____ is the philosophy of Karl Marx, which he formulated by taking the dialectic of Hegel and joining it to the Materialism of Feuerbach. According to many followers of Karl Marx's thinking, it is the philosophical basis of Marxism.

_____ was coined in 1887 by Joseph Dietzgen, a socialist tanner who corresponded with Marx both during and after the failed 1848 German Revolution.

   a. Dialectical materialism   b. Differential and Absolute Ground Rent
   c. Grundrisse   d. Proletarian internationalism

34. _____ is the political philosophy and practice derived from the work of Karl Marx and Friedrich Engels. _____ holds at its core a critical analysis of capitalism and a theory of social change. The powerful and innovative methods of analysis introduced by Marx have been very influential in a broad range of disciplines.
   a. Adam Smith   b. Karl Heinrich Marx
   c. Marxism   d. Neo-Gramscianism

35. _____ Abd al-Majid al-Tikriti was the President of Iraq from July 16, 1979 until April 9, 2003.

A leading member of the revolutionary Ba'ath Party, which espoused secular pan-Arabism, economic modernization, and Arab socialism, Saddam played a key role in the 1968 coup that brought the party to long-term power. As vice president under the ailing General Ahmed Hassan al-Bakr, Saddam tightly controlled conflict between the government and the armed forces--at a time when many other groups were considered capable of overthrowing the government--by creating repressive security forces.

Chapter 6. Socialism as an Economic System

a. Adam Smith
b. Adolph Fischer
c. Adolf Hitler
d. Saddam Hussein

36. Economics:

- _____ ,the desire to own something and the ability to pay for it
- _____ curve,a graphic representation of a _____ schedule
- _____ deposit, the money in checking accounts
- _____ pull theory,the theory that inflation occurs when _____ for goods and services exceeds existing supplies
- _____ schedule,a table that lists the quantity of a good a person will buy it each different price
- _____ side economics,the school of economics at believes government spending and tax cuts open economy by raising _____

a. Demand
b. Variability
c. Production
d. McKesson ' Robbins scandal

37. _____ s is the social science that studies the production, distribution, and consumption of goods and services. The term _____ s comes from the Ancient Greek oá¼°κονομῖα from oá¼¶κος (oikos, 'house') + vĭŒµος (nomos, 'custom' or 'law'), hence 'rules of the house(hold)'. Current _____ models developed out of the broader field of political economy in the late 19th century, owing to a desire to use an empirical approach more akin to the physical sciences.

a. Economic
b. Energy economics
c. Inflation
d. Opportunity cost

38. The _____ was a law of economics that asserted that real wages in the long run would trend toward the value needed to keep the workers' population constant. The alleged law was named and popularized by the German socialist Ferdinand Lassalle in the mid 1800s.

According to Lassalle, wages cannot fall below subsistence level because without subsistence, laborers will be unable to work for long.

a. Celler-Kefauver Act
b. Permanent Normal Trade Relations
c. Duty of fair representation
d. Subsistence theory of wages

39. _____ is an economic model based on price, utility and quantity in a market. It predicts that in a competitive market, price will function to equalize the quantity demanded by consumers, and the quantity supplied by producers, resulting in an economic equilibrium of price and quantity. The model incorporates other factors changing equilibrium as a shift of demand and/or supply.

a. Rational addiction
b. Deferred gratification
c. Supply and demand
d. Joint demand

40. The impact of the Mexican economic crisis on the Southern Cone and Brazil was labeled the _____ .

The crisis is also known in Spanish as el error de diciembre -- The December Mistake-- a term coined by the then ex-president Carlos Salinas de Gortari. While these critics agree that a devaluation was necessary, they argue that the way it was handled was politically incorrect .

- a. 130-30 fund
- b. 1921 recession
- c. 100-year flood
- d. Tequila effect

41. _____ was a global military conflict which involved a majority of the world's nations, including all of the great powers, organized into two opposing military alliances: the Allies and the Axis. The war involved the mobilization of over 100 million military personnel, making it the most widespread war in history. In a state of 'total war', the major participants placed their entire economic, industrial, and scientific capabilities at the service of the war effort, erasing the distinction between civilian and military resources.
- a. World War II
- b. 100-year flood
- c. 1921 recession
- d. 130-30 fund

42. The _____ was an early English joint-stock company that was formed initially for pursuing trade with the East Indies, but that ended up trading with the Indian subcontinent and China. The oldest among several similarly formed European East India Companies, the Company was granted an English Royal Charter, under the name Governor and Company of Merchants of London Trading into the East Indies, by Elizabeth I on 31 December 1600. After a rival English company challenged its monopoly in the late 17th century, the two companies were merged in 1708 to form the United Company of Merchants of England Trading to the East Indies, commonly styled the Honourable _____, and abbreviated, HEast India Company; the Company was colloquially referred to as John Company, and in India as Company Bahadur .
- a. East India Company
- b. AD-IA Model
- c. ACCRA Cost of Living Index
- d. ACEA agreement

43. The _____ , 1949-1991, was an economic organization of communist states and a kind of Eastern Bloc equivalent to--but more geographically inclusive than--the European Economic Community. The military equivalent to the Comecon was the Warsaw Pact, though Comecon's membership was significantly wider. The Comecon was the Eastern Bloc's reply to the formation of the OEEC .
- a. 130-30 fund
- b. 100-year flood
- c. Council for Mutual Economic Assistance
- d. 1921 recession

44. The term _____ refers to economy-wide fluctuations in production or economic activity over several months or years. These fluctuations occur around a long-term growth trend, and typically involve shifts over time between periods of relatively rapid economic growth (expansion or boom), and periods of relative stagnation or decline (contraction or recession.)

These fluctuations are often measured using the growth rate of real gross domestic product.

- a. Tobit model
- b. Consumer theory
- c. Nominal value
- d. Business cycle

45. _____ is the theory which attributes primacy to the economic structure over politics in the development of human history. It is usually associated with the theories of Karl Marx, although many Marxist thinkers have dismissed plain and unilateral _____ as a form of 'vulgar Marxism', or 'economism', nowhere included in Marx's works.

Chapter 6. Socialism as an Economic System

_____ as understood by vulgar Marxism is the positivist belief that economical laws determine the course of history, in the same way that Auguste Comte considered that laws governed society.

a. ACCRA Cost of Living Index
b. AD-IA Model
c. ACEA agreement
d. Economic determinism

46. The term '_____' refers to the concept of collecting information and attempting to spot a pattern in the information. In some fields of study, the term '_____' has more formally-defined meanings.

In project management _____ is a mathematical technique that uses historical results to predict future outcome.

a. Quantile regression
b. Trend analysis
c. Coefficient of determination
d. Probit model

47. _____ is the study of questions about the city, government, politics, liberty, justice, property, rights, law and the enforcement of a legal code by authority: what they are, why (or even if) they are needed, what makes a government legitimate, what rights and freedoms it should protect and why, what form it should take and why, what the law is, and what duties citizens owe to a legitimate government, if any, and when it may be legitimately overthrown--if ever. In a vernacular sense, the term '_____' often refers to a general view, or specific ethic, political belief or attitude, about politics that does not necessarily belong to the technical discipline of philosophy.

_____ can also be understood by analysing it through the perspectives of metaphysics, epistemology and axiology thereby unearthing the ultimate reality side, the knowledge or methodical side and the value aspects of politics.

a. Global justice
b. Materialism
c. Deductive logic
d. Political philosophy

48. _____ theory is a doctrine of military ethics of Roman philosophical and Catholic origin studied by moral theologians, ethicists and international policy makers which holds that a conflict can and ought to meet the criteria of philosophical, religious or political justice, provided it follows certain conditions.

The idea that resorting to war can only be just under certain conditions goes back at least to Cicero. However its importance is connected to Christian medieval theory beginning from Augustine of Hippo and Thomas Aquinas.

a. 130-30 fund
b. 1921 recession
c. 100-year flood
d. Just War

49. _____ is a type of trade policy that allows traders to act and transact without interference from government. Thus, the policy permits trading partners mutual gains from trade, with goods and services produced according to the theory of comparative advantage.

Chapter 6. Socialism as an Economic System

Under a _____ policy, prices are a reflection of true supply and demand, and are the sole determinant of resource allocation.

a. 100-year flood
c. Free Trade
b. 1921 recession
d. 130-30 fund

50. _____ is a designated group of countries that have agreed to eliminate tariffs, quotas and preferences on most (if not all) goods and services traded between them. It can be considered the second stage of economic integration. Countries choose this kind of economic integration form if their economical structures are complementary.
a. MERCOSUR
c. 100-year flood
b. 130-30 fund
d. Free Trade Area

51. An _____ or Å"conomic system is a system that involves the production, distribution and consumption of goods and services between the entities in a particular society. It is the method used by society to produce and distribute goods and services. The _____ is composed of people and institutions, including their relationships to productive resources, such as through the convention of property.
a. Information economy
c. Intention economy
b. Economic system
d. Indicative planning

52. In mathematics, a _____ is a constant multiplicative factor of a certain object. For example, in the expression $9x^2$, the _____ of x^2 is 9.

The object can be such things as a variable, a vector, a function, etc.

a. 1921 recession
c. 100-year flood
b. Coefficient
d. 130-30 fund

53. Economic interventionism or _____ is an action in a Market economy taken by a government, beyond the basic regulation of fraud and enforcement of contracts, in an effort to affect its own economy. Economic intervention can be aimed at a variety of political or economic objectives, such as promoting economic growth, increasing employment, raising wages, raising or reducing prices, promoting equality, managing the money supply and interest rates, increasing profits, or addressing market failures. The intervention may to direct, or indirect as in the case of indicative planning.
a. Economic planning
c. AD-IA Model
b. ACCRA Cost of Living Index
d. ACEA agreement

54. The _____ of 1938 (_____, ch. 676, 52 Stat. 1060, June 25, 1938, 29 U.S.C.ch.8), also called the Wages and Hours Bill, is United States federal law that applies to employees engaged in interstate commerce or employed by an enterprise engaged in commerce or in the production of goods for commerce, unless the employer can claim an exemption from coverage.
a. Habitability
c. Fair Labor Standards Act
b. Hostile work environment
d. Generalized System of Preferences

Chapter 6. Socialism as an Economic System

55. A _____ is a group of people who share or are motivated by at least one common issue or interest, or work together on a specific project(s) to achieve a common objective. _____s are also characterised by attempts to share and exercise political and social power and to make decisions on a consensus-driven and egalitarian basis. _____s differ from cooperatives in that they are not necessarily focused upon an economic benefit or saving (but can be that as well.)
   a. 130-30 fund
   b. 1921 recession
   c. 100-year flood
   d. Collective

56. Collective farming is an organization of agricultural production in which the holdings of several farmers are run as a joint enterprise. A _____ is essentially an agricultural production cooperative in which members-owners engage jointly in farming activities. Typical examples of _____s are the kolkhozy that dominated Soviet agriculture between 1930 and 1992 and the Israeli kibbutzim.
   a. 100-year flood
   b. 1921 recession
   c. 130-30 fund
   d. Collective farm

57. _____ is a dystopian novel by George Orwell. Published in England on 17 August 1945, the book reflects events leading up to and during the Stalin era before World War II. Orwell, a democratic socialist and a member of the Independent Labour Party for many years, was a critic of Joseph Stalin and was suspicious of Moscow-directed Stalinism after his experiences with the NKVD during the Spanish Civil War.
   a. Adolph Fischer
   b. Animal Farm
   c. Adam Smith
   d. Adolf Hitler

58. _____ is the name given to the principles of internal organization used by Leninist political parties, and the term is sometimes used as a synonym for any Leninist policy inside a political party. The democratic aspect of this organizational method describes the freedom of members of the political party to discuss and debate matters of policy and direction, but once the decision of the party is made by majority vote, all members are expected to uphold that decision. This latter aspect represents the centralism.
   a. Religious communism
   b. Social fascism
   c. Communist League
   d. Democratic centralism

Chapter 7. The Rise and Fall of Communism

1. _____ is a socioeconomic structure and political ideology that promotes the establishment of an egalitarian, classless, stateless society based on common ownership and control of the means of production and property in general. In political science, the term '_____' is sometimes used to refer to communist states, a form of government in which the state operates under a one-party system and declares allegiance to Marxism-Leninism or a derivative thereof, even if the party does not actually claim that it has already reached _____.

Forerunners of communist ideas existed in antiquity and particularly in the 18th and early 19th century France, with thinkers such as Jean-Jacques Rousseau and the more radical Gracchus Babeuf.

- a. Communism
- b. New Communist Movement
- c. Social fascism
- d. Democratic centralism

2. _____, originally also Bolshevists were a faction of the Marxist Russian Social Democratic Labour Party which split apart from the Menshevik faction at the Second Party Congress in 1903 and ultimately became the Communist Party of the Soviet Union. The _____ seized power in Russia during the October Revolution phase of the Russian Revolution of 1917, and founded the Soviet Union.

_____ were an organization of professional revolutionaries under a strict internal hierarchy governed by the principle of democratic centralism and quasi-military discipline, who considered themselves as a vanguard of the revolutionary proletariat.

- a. Commodity form theory
- b. Bolsheviks
- c. Redistribution game
- d. Real socialism

3. _____s is the social science that studies the production, distribution, and consumption of goods and services. The term _____s comes from the Ancient Greek οá¼°κονομῖα from οá¼¶κος (oikos, 'house') + vĺŒμος (nomos, 'custom' or 'law'), hence 'rules of the house(hold)'. Current _____ models developed out of the broader field of political economy in the late 19th century, owing to a desire to use an empirical approach more akin to the physical sciences.
- a. Inflation
- b. Energy economics
- c. Opportunity cost
- d. Economic

4. _____ refers to the actions that governments take in the economic field. It covers the systems for setting interest rates and government deficit as well as the labour market, national ownership, and many other areas of government.

Such policies are often influenced by international institutions like the International Monetary Fund or World Bank as well as political beliefs and the consequent policies of parties.

- a. ACEA agreement
- b. AD-IA Model
- c. ACCRA Cost of Living Index
- d. Economic Policy

5. The _____ was an economic policy proposed by Vladimir Lenin to prevent the Russian economy from collapsing. Allowing some private ventures, the _____ allowed small businesses/shop for instant to reopen for private profit while the state continued to control banks, foreign trade, and large industries. It was officially decided in the course of the 10th Congress of the All-Russian Communist Party.
- a. Trade adjustment assistance
- b. New Economic Policy
- c. Delancey Street Foundation
- d. Financial Crimes Enforcement Network

6. _____ was the last Emperor of Russia, Grand Duke of Finland, and claimed the title of King of Poland. His official title was _____, Emperor and Autocrat of All the Russias and he is currently regarded as Saint Nicholas the Passion Bearer by the Russian Orthodox Church.

_____ ruled from 1894 until his abdication on 15 March 1917.

   a. Maximilian Carl Emil Weber
   b. Werner Sombart
   c. George Cabot Lodge II
   d. Nicholas II

7. The _____ , 1949-1991, was an economic organization of communist states and a kind of Eastern Bloc equivalent to--but more geographically inclusive than--the European Economic Community. The military equivalent to the Comecon was the Warsaw Pact, though Comecon's membership was significantly wider. The Comecon was the Eastern Bloc's reply to the formation of the OEEC .
   a. 130-30 fund
   b. 1921 recession
   c. 100-year flood
   d. Council for Mutual Economic Assistance

8. The _____ was a revolution and a part of the Russian Revolution--that began with an armed insurrection in Petrograd traditionally dated to 25 October 1917 Julian calendar . It was the second phase of the overall Russian Revolution of 1917, after the February Revolution of the same year. The _____ overthrew the Russian Provisional Government and gave the power to the Soviets dominated by Bolsheviks.
   a. AD-IA Model
   b. ACEA agreement
   c. October Revolution
   d. ACCRA Cost of Living Index

9. _____ the Great War, and the War to End All Wars, was a global military conflict which involved the majority of the world's great powers, organized into two opposing military alliances: the Entente Powers and the Central Powers. Over 70 million military personnel were mobilized in one of the largest wars in history. In a state of total war, the major combatants fully placed their scientific and industrial capabilities at the service of the war effort.
   a. 130-30 fund
   b. 1921 recession
   c. 100-year flood
   d. World War I

10. An _____ or Å"conomic system is a system that involves the production, distribution and consumption of goods and services between the entities in a particular society. It is the method used by society to produce and distribute goods and services. The _____ is composed of people and institutions, including their relationships to productive resources, such as through the convention of property.
   a. Indicative planning
   b. Intention economy
   c. Economic system
   d. Information economy

11. A political party described as a _____ includes those that advocate the application of the social principles of communism through a communist form of government. The name originates from the 1848 tract Manifesto of the _____ by Karl Marx, Friedrich Engels. The Leninist concept of a _____ encompases a larger political system and includes not only an ideological orientation but also a wide set of organizational policies.
   a. Communism
   b. Communist Party
   c. Criticisms of anarcho-capitalism
   d. Criticisms of Communist party rule

Chapter 7. The Rise and Fall of Communism

12. _____ was a leader of the Soviet Union, serving as General Secretary of the Communist Party of the Soviet Union from 1953 to 1964, following the death of Joseph Stalin, and Chairman of the Council of Ministers from 1958 to 1964. Khrushchev was responsible for the partial de-Stalinization of the Soviet Union, for backing the progress of the world's early space program, as well as for several relatively liberal reforms ranging from agriculture to foreign policy. Khrushchev's party colleagues removed him from power in 1964, replacing him with Leonid Brezhnev.

Khrushchev was born in Kalinovka, a town in what is now Russia's Kursk Oblast, to parents of Russian origin.

   a. Adolf Hitler
   b. Nikita Sergeyevich Khrushchev
   c. Adam Smith
   d. Adolph Fischer

13. _____ was a global military conflict which involved a majority of the world's nations, including all of the great powers, organized into two opposing military alliances: the Allies and the Axis. The war involved the mobilization of over 100 million military personnel, making it the most widespread war in history. In a state of 'total war', the major participants placed their entire economic, industrial, and scientific capabilities at the service of the war effort, erasing the distinction between civilian and military resources.

   a. 1921 recession
   b. 130-30 fund
   c. 100-year flood
   d. World War II

14. _____ in political thought refers to economic theories of social organization advocating collective ownership and administration of the means of production and distribution of goods, and a society characterized by equality for all individuals, with an egalitarian method of compensation. Modern _____ originated in the late 19th-century intellectual and working class political movement that criticized the effects of industrialization and private ownership on society. Karl Marx posited that _____ would be achieved via class struggle and a proletarian revolution after a transitional stage from capitalism called the dictatorship of the proletariat.

   a. Adam Smith
   b. Adolph Fischer
   c. Adolf Hitler
   d. Socialism

15.

_____ was the last General Secretary of the Communist Party of the Soviet Union, serving from 1985 until 1991, and also the last head of state of the USSR, serving from 1988 until its collapse in 1991. He was the only Soviet leader to have been born after the October Revolution of 1917.

Gorbachev was born in Stavropol Krai into a peasant family, and operated combine harvesters on collective farms.

   a. Adolf Hitler
   b. Adam Smith
   c. Mikhail Sergeyevich Gorbachev
   d. Adolph Fischer

16. The _____ is a measure of statistical dispersion, commonly used as a measure of inequality of income distribution or inequality of wealth distribution. It is defined as a ratio with values between 0 and 1: A low _____ indicates more equal income or wealth distribution, while a high _____ indicates more unequal distribution. 0 corresponds to perfect equality (everyone having exactly the same income) and 1 corresponds to perfect inequality (where one person has all the income, while everyone else has zero income.)

Chapter 7. The Rise and Fall of Communism

a. Gini coefficient
b. Compensating variation
c. Suits index
d. Leapfrogging

17. In mathematics, a _____ is a constant multiplicative factor of a certain object. For example, in the expression $9x^2$, the _____ of x^2 is 9.

The object can be such things as a variable, a vector, a function, etc.

a. 100-year flood
b. 130-30 fund
c. 1921 recession
d. Coefficient

18. The _____ is a document that legalized the creation of a union of several Soviet republics in the form of the Union of Soviet Socialist Republics. The Declaration of the Creation of the USSR was also issued; it may be considered a political preamble to the Treaty.

On December 29, 1922, a conference of delegations from the Russian SFSR, the Transcaucasian SFSR, the Ukrainian SSR and the Byelorussian SSR approved the Treaty of Creation of the USSR and the Declaration of the Creation of the USSR, these two documents were confirmed by the 1st Congress of Soviets of the USSR and signed by heads of delegations - Mikhail Kalinin, Mikha Tskhakaya, Mikhail Frunze and Grigory Petrovsky, Aleksandr Chervyakov respectively on December 30, 1922.

a. 100-year flood
b. 130-30 fund
c. 1921 recession
d. Treaty on the Creation of the USSR

19. _____ is the transition to a more democratic political regime. It may be the transition from an authoritarian regime to a full democracy or transition from a semi-authoritarian political system to a democratic political system. The outcome may be consolidated or _____ may face frequent reversals (as it has faced for example in Argentina.)

a. 100-year flood
b. 1921 recession
c. Democratization
d. 130-30 fund

20. _____ is a form of nationalism wherein the 'nation' is defined in terms of ethnicity. Whatever specific ethnicity is involved, _____ always includes some element of descent from previous generations. Furthermore, the central theme of ethnic nationalists is that '...nations are defined by a shared heritage, which usually includes a common language, a common faith, and a common ethnic ancestry.'It also includes ideas of a culture shared between members of the group, and with their ancestors, and usually a shared language; however it is different from purely cultural definitions of 'the nation' (which allow people to become members of a nation by cultural assimilation) and a purely linguistic definitions

a. ACEA agreement
b. ACCRA Cost of Living Index
c. AD-IA Model
d. Ethnic nationalism

21. _____ is the increase in the amount of the goods and services produced by an economy over time. It is conventionally measured as the percent rate of increase in real gross domestic product, or real GDP. Growth is usually calculated in real terms, i.e. inflation-adjusted terms, in order to net out the effect of inflation on the price of the goods and services produced.

a. ACEA agreement
b. ACCRA Cost of Living Index
c. AD-IA Model
d. Economic growth

Chapter 7. The Rise and Fall of Communism

22. _____: Kritik der politischen Ökonomie is an extensive treatise on political economy written in German by Karl Marx and edited in part by Friedrich Engels. The book is a critical analysis of capitalism. Its first volume was published in 1867.
   a. Dialectics of Nature
   b. Das Kapital
   c. Capital accumulation
   d. Productive force

23. The _____ is a region that spans southwestern Asia and northeastern Africa. It has no clear boundaries, often used as a synonym to Near East, in opposition to Far East. The term '_____' was popularized around 1900 in the United Kingdom.
   a. 1921 recession
   b. 100-year flood
   c. Middle East
   d. 130-30 fund

24. _____ is money accepted for exchange of goods in an economy. The prevalence of one money over another arises, usually, when a government designates through decrees that the government shall accept only particular notes and coins in payment for taxes. Typically, money of _____ consists of stamped coins and minted paper bills.
   a. Security thread
   b. Local currency
   c. Totnes pound
   d. Currency

25. _____ is that which is owed; usually referencing assets owed, but the term can also cover moral obligations and other interactions not requiring money. In the case of assets, _____ is a means of using future purchasing power in the present before a summation has been earned. Some companies and corporations use _____ as a part of their overall corporate finance strategy.
   a. Hard money loan
   b. Debenture
   c. Collateral Management
   d. Debt

26. _____ or strong currency, in economics, refers to a globally traded currency that can serve as a reliable and stable store of value. Factors contributing to a currency's hard status can include political stability, low inflation, consistent monetary and fiscal policies, backing by reserves of precious metals, and long-term stable or upward-trending valuation against other currencies on a trade-weighted basis.

As of 2008, hard currencies could be argued to include the United States dollar, euro, Swiss franc, British pound sterling, Norwegian krone, Swedish krona, Canadian dollar, Japanese yen, and Australian dollar.

   a. Devaluation
   b. Store of value
   c. Convertibility
   d. Hard currency

27. The _____ is a regional organization whose participating countries are former Soviet Republics.

The CIS is comparable to a confederation similar to the original European Community. Although the CIS has few supranational powers, it is more than a purely symbolic organization, possessing coordinating powers in the realm of trade, finance, lawmaking, and security.

   a. 130-30 fund
   b. 100-year flood
   c. 1921 recession
   d. Commonwealth of Independent States

Chapter 7. The Rise and Fall of Communism

28. _____ is a type of trade policy that allows traders to act and transact without interference from government. Thus, the policy permits trading partners mutual gains from trade, with goods and services produced according to the theory of comparative advantage.

Under a _____ policy, prices are a reflection of true supply and demand, and are the sole determinant of resource allocation.

   a. 1921 recession
   b. 130-30 fund
   c. 100-year flood
   d. Free Trade

29. The _____ is a trilateral trade bloc in North America created by the governments of the United States, Canada, and Mexico. The agreement creating the trade bloc came into force on January 1, 1994. It superseded the Canada-United States Free Trade Agreement between the U.S. and Canada.
   a. North American Free Trade Agreement
   b. Federal Reserve Bank Notes
   c. Case-Shiller Home Price Indices
   d. Demand-side technologies

30. The _____ was an early English joint-stock company that was formed initially for pursuing trade with the East Indies, but that ended up trading with the Indian subcontinent and China. The oldest among several similarly formed European East India Companies, the Company was granted an English Royal Charter, under the name Governor and Company of Merchants of London Trading into the East Indies, by Elizabeth I on 31 December 1600. After a rival English company challenged its monopoly in the late 17th century, the two companies were merged in 1708 to form the United Company of Merchants of England Trading to the East Indies, commonly styled the Honourable _____, and abbreviated, HEast India Company; the Company was colloquially referred to as John Company, and in India as Company Bahadur .
   a. AD-IA Model
   b. ACEA agreement
   c. ACCRA Cost of Living Index
   d. East India Company

31. _____ is the structure and set of regulations in place to control activity, usually in large organizations and government. As opposed to adhocracy, it is represented by standardized procedure (rule-following) that dictates the execution of most or all processes within the body, formal division of powers, hierarchy, and relationships. In practice the interpretation and execution of policy can lead to informal influence.
   a. 100-year flood
   b. 1921 recession
   c. Bureaucracy
   d. 130-30 fund

32. The _____ is an international organization that oversees the global financial system by following the macroeconomic policies of its member countries, in particular those with an impact on exchange rates and the balance of payments. It is an organization formed to stabilize international exchange rates and facilitate development. It also offers financial and technical assistance to its members, making it an international lender of last resort.
   a. Office of Thrift Supervision
   b. ACEA agreement
   c. ACCRA Cost of Living Index
   d. International Monetary Fund

33. The post-Soviet states, also commonly known as the _____ or former Soviet republics, are the 15 independent nations that split off from the Union of Soviet Socialist Republics in its breakup in December 1991. Excluding the Baltic states (which were independent before World War II and already in 1989 signalled their political intention to dissociate themselves from the rest of the Soviet Union), they were also referred to as the Newly Independent States (NIS.) Post-Soviet states in English alphabetical order:1.

Chapter 7. The Rise and Fall of Communism

a. 100-year flood
b. 1921 recession
c. 130-30 fund
d. Former Soviet Union

34. _____ refers to the movement of cash into or out of a business or financial product. It is usually measured during a specified, finite period of time. Measurement of _____ can be used

- to determine a project's rate of return or value. The time of _____s into and out of projects are used as inputs in financial models such as internal rate of return, and net present value.
- to determine problems with a business's liquidity. Being profitable does not necessarily mean being liquid. A company can fail because of a shortage of cash, even while profitable.
- as an alternate measure of a business's profits when it is believed that accrual accounting concepts do not represent economic realities. For example, a company may be notionally profitable but generating little operational cash (as may be the case for a company that barters its products rather than selling for cash.) In such a case, the company may be deriving additional operating cash by issuing shares evaluating default risk, re-investment requirements, etc.

_____ is a generic term used differently depending on the context. It may be defined by users for their own purposes.

a. Cash flow
b. Strip financing
c. Restricted stock
d. Second lien loan

35. The _____ was a research project conducted in the early 1980s. The project's principal aim was to learn about the life in the Soviet Union, which in turn would contribute to the disciplines of Sovietology, political science, economics and sociology.

The study had three principal goals:

- Conducting a study of contemporary Soviet society based upon interviews with recent immigrants now living in the United States.
- Promoting the involvement of young scholars so that the field of Soviet studies developed.
- Making the data and research products developed available to all interested scholars.

The _____ had its origins in a meeting at the Kennan Institute in August 1979, where senior academic scholars and U.S. government specialists discussed the feasibility of such a project. One of the main obstacles was the 'Kissinger rule' and a design phase proposal was funded by the National Council for Soviet and East European Research in November 1979.

a. 130-30 fund
b. Soviet Interview Project
c. 1921 recession
d. 100-year flood

36. In economics _____ is defined as the sum of private and external costs. Economic theorists ascribe individual decision-making to a calculation costs and benefits. Rational choice theory assumes that individuals only consider their own private costs when making decisions, not the costs that may be borne by others.

a. Khozraschyot
b. Cost-Volume-Profit Analysis
c. Psychic cost
d. Social cost

Chapter 8. The Russian Federation

1. A political party described as a _____ includes those that advocate the application of the social principles of communism through a communist form of government. The name originates from the 1848 tract Manifesto of the _____ by Karl Marx, Friedrich Engels. The Leninist concept of a _____ encompasses a larger political system and includes not only an ideological orientation but also a wide set of organizational policies.
   - a. Criticisms of Communist party rule
   - b. Criticisms of anarcho-capitalism
   - c. Communism
   - d. Communist Party

2. _____ is a dystopian novel by George Orwell. Published in England on 17 August 1945, the book reflects events leading up to and during the Stalin era before World War II. Orwell, a democratic socialist and a member of the Independent Labour Party for many years, was a critic of Joseph Stalin and was suspicious of Moscow-directed Stalinism after his experiences with the NKVD during the Spanish Civil War.
   - a. Adolf Hitler
   - b. Adolph Fischer
   - c. Animal Farm
   - d. Adam Smith

3. _____ is a broad label that refers to any individuals or households that use goods and services generated within the economy. The concept of a _____ is used in different contexts, so that the usage and significance of the term may vary.

   Typically when business people and economists talk of _____s they are talking about person as _____, an aggregated commodity item with little individuality other than that expressed in the buy/not-buy decision.

   - a. 100-year flood
   - b. 1921 recession
   - c. 130-30 fund
   - d. Consumer

4. The Great Proletarian _____ in the People's Republic of China was a period of widespread social and political upheaval; the nation-wide chaos and economic disarray engulfed much of Chinese society between 1966 and 1976.

   It was launched by Mao Zedong, the chairman of the Communist Party of China, on May 16, 1966, who alleged that liberal bourgeoisie elements were dominating the party and insisted that they needed to be removed through post-revolutionary class struggle by mobilizing the thoughts and actions of China's youth, who formed Red Guards groups around the country. Although Mao himself officially declared the _____ to have ended in 1969, today it is widely believed that the power struggles and political instability between 1969 and the arrest of the Gang of Four as well as the death of Mao in 1976 were also part of the Revolution.

   - a. 1921 recession
   - b. 130-30 fund
   - c. Cultural Revolution
   - d. 100-year flood

5. _____, in law and economics, is a form of risk management primarily used to hedge against the risk of a contingent loss. _____ is defined as the equitable transfer of the risk of a loss, from one entity to another, in exchange for a premium, and can be thought of as a guaranteed small loss to prevent a large, possibly devastating loss. An insurer is a company selling the _____; an insured or policyholder is the person or entity buying the _____.
   - a. Insurance
   - b. ACCRA Cost of Living Index
   - c. AD-IA Model
   - d. ACEA agreement

6. Competition law, known in the United States as _____ law, has three main elements:

- prohibiting agreements or practices that restrict free trading and competition between business entities. This includes in particular the repression of cartels.
- banning abusive behaviour by a firm dominating a market, or anti-competitive practices that tend to lead to such a dominant position. Practices controlled in this way may include predatory pricing, tying, price gouging, refusal to deal, and many others.
- supervising the mergers and acquisitions of large corporations, including some joint ventures. Transactions that are considered to threaten the competitive process can be prohibited altogether, or approved subject to 'remedies' such as an obligation to divest part of the merged business or to offer licences or access to facilities to enable other businesses to continue competing.

The substance and practice of competition law varies from jurisdiction to jurisdiction. Protecting the interests of consumers (consumer welfare) and ensuring that entrepreneurs have an opportunity to compete in the market economy are often treated as important objectives. Competition law is closely connected with law on deregulation of access to markets, state aids and subsidies, the privatisation of state owned assets and the establishment of independent sector regulators. In recent decades, competition law has been viewed as a way to provide better public services.

a. Anti-Inflation Act
b. Antitrust
c. Intellectual property law
d. United Kingdom competition law

7. _____ is a legally declared inability or impairment of ability of an individual or organization to pay its creditors. Creditors may file a _____ petition against a debtor ('involuntary _____') in an effort to recoup a portion of what they are owed or initiate a restructuring. In the majority of cases, however, _____ is initiated by the debtor (a 'voluntary _____' that is filed by the insolvent individual or organization.)

a. Bankruptcy in the United Kingdom
b. Petition mill
c. Liquidation
d. Bankruptcy

8. _____, known in the United States as antitrust law, has three main elements:

- prohibiting agreements or practices that restrict free trading and competition between business entities. This includes in particular the repression of cartels.
- banning abusive behaviour by a firm dominating a market, or anti-competitive practices that tend to lead to such a dominant position. Practices controlled in this way may include predatory pricing, tying, price gouging, refusal to deal, and many others.
- supervising the mergers and acquisitions of large corporations, including some joint ventures. Transactions that are considered to threaten the competitive process can be prohibited altogether, or approved subject to 'remedies' such as an obligation to divest part of the merged business or to offer licences or access to facilities to enable other businesses to continue competing.

The substance and practice of _____ varies from jurisdiction to jurisdiction. Protecting the interests of consumers (consumer welfare) and ensuring that entrepreneurs have an opportunity to compete in the market economy are often treated as important objectives. _____ is closely connected with law on deregulation of access to markets, state aids and subsidies, the privatisation of state owned assets and the establishment of independent sector regulators. In recent decades, _____ has been viewed as a way to provide better public services.

    a. Hostile work environment
    b. Fee simple
    c. Competition law
    d. Due diligence

9. _____ are legal property rights over creations of the mind, both artistic and commercial, and the corresponding fields of law. Under _____ law, owners are granted certain exclusive rights to a variety of intangible assets, such as musical, literary, and artistic works; ideas, discoveries and inventions; and words, phrases, symbols, and designs. Common types of _____ include copyrights, trademarks, patents, industrial design rights and trade secrets.

    a. Expedited Funds Availability Act
    b. Independent contractor
    c. Ease of Doing Business Index
    d. Intellectual property

10. Intellectual property (IP) are legal property rights over creations of the mind, both artistic and commercial, and the corresponding fields of law. Under _____, owners are granted certain exclusive rights to a variety of intangible assets, such as musical, literary, and artistic works; ideas, discoveries and inventions; and words, phrases, symbols, and designs. Common types of intellectual property include copyrights, trademarks, patents, industrial design rights and trade secrets.

    a. Intellectual property law
    b. ATR.1 certificate
    c. Internet Tax Freedom Act
    d. Ease of Doing Business Index

11. A _____ is an economy based on the division of labor in which the prices of goods and services are determined in a free price system set by supply and demand. This is often contrasted with a planned economy, in which a central government determines the price of goods and services using a fixed price system. Market economies are contrasted with mixed economy where the price system is not entirely free but under some government control that is not extensive enough to constitute a planned economy.

    a. Market economy
    b. Network Economy
    c. Nutritional Economics
    d. Commons-based peer production

12. A security is a fungible, negotiable instrument representing financial value. _____ are broadly categorized into debt _____; equity _____, e.g., common stocks; and derivative (finance) contracts such as forwards, futures, options and swaps. The company or other entity issuing the security is called the issuer.

    a. Pass-Through Certificates
    b. Red herring prospectus
    c. Settlement risk
    d. Securities

13. The _____ established under Napoléon I in 1804. It was drafted rapidly by a commission of four eminent jurists and entered into force on March 21, 1804. Even though the _____ was not the first legal code to be established in a European country with a civil legal system -- it was preceded by the Codex Maximilianeus bavaricus civilis (Bavaria, 1756), the Allgemeines Landrecht and the West Galician Code, -- it is considered the first successful codification and strongly influenced the law of many other countries.

a. Holder in due course
b. Big Boy Letter
c. Leave of absence
d. Napoleonic code

14. The Communist Party of Peru, more commonly known as the _____ , is a Pseudo-Maoist guerrilla organization in Peru. When it first launched the internal conflict in Peru in 1980, its stated goal was to replace what it saw as bourgeois democracy with 'New Democracy.' The _____ believed that by imposing a dictatorship of the proletariat, inducing cultural revolution, and eventually sparking world revolution, they could arrive at pure communism. The _____ also believed that all existing socialist countries were revisionist, and that the _____ itself was the vanguard of the world communist movement.
   a. Shining Path
   b. 100-year flood
   c. 1921 recession
   d. 130-30 fund

15. _____ is the belief that changes occur, or ought to occur, slowly in the form of gradual steps

In politics, the concept of _____ is used to describe the belief that change ought to be modified in small, discrete increments rather than abrupt changes such as revolutions or uprisings. _____ is one of the defining features of political conservatism and reformism. According to Machiavellian politics, Congressmen are pushed to agree to _____.

   a. Gradualism
   b. 130-30 fund
   c. 100-year flood
   d. 1921 recession

16. _____ is the incidence or process of transferring ownership of a business, enterprise, agency or public service from the public sector (government) to the private sector (business.) In a broader sense, _____ refers to transfer of any government function to the private sector including governmental functions like revenue collection and law enforcement.

The term '_____' also has been used to describe two unrelated transactions.

   a. Compound empowerment
   b. Privatization
   c. Performance reports
   d. Ricardian equivalence

17. A _____ is a bond which is worth a certain monetary value and which may only be spent for specific reasons or on specific goods. Examples include -- but are not limited to -- housing, travel and food _____s. The term _____ is also a synonym for receipt, and is often used to refer to receipts used as evidence of, for example, the declaration that a service has been performed or that an expenditure has been made.
   a. 100-year flood
   b. 130-30 fund
   c. Voucher
   d. 1921 recession

18. The _____ of 1938 (_____, ch. 676, 52 Stat. 1060, June 25, 1938, 29 U.S.C.ch.8), also called the Wages and Hours Bill, is United States federal law that applies to employees engaged in interstate commerce or employed by an enterprise engaged in commerce or in the production of goods for commerce, unless the employer can claim an exemption from coverage.
   a. Generalized System of Preferences
   b. Hostile work environment
   c. Habitability
   d. Fair Labor Standards Act

19. A _____ is a group of people who share or are motivated by at least one common issue or interest, or work together on a specific project(s) to achieve a common objective. _____s are also characterised by attempts to share and exercise political and social power and to make decisions on a consensus-driven and egalitarian basis. _____s differ from cooperatives in that they are not necessarily focused upon an economic benefit or saving (but can be that as well.)
- a. 1921 recession
- b. Collective
- c. 100-year flood
- d. 130-30 fund

20. Collective farming is an organization of agricultural production in which the holdings of several farmers are run as a joint enterprise. A _____ is essentially an agricultural production cooperative in which members-owners engage jointly in farming activities. Typical examples of _____s are the kolkhozy that dominated Soviet agriculture between 1930 and 1992 and the Israeli kibbutzim.
- a. 130-30 fund
- b. 1921 recession
- c. 100-year flood
- d. Collective farm

21. In economics, a _____ is a mechanism that allows people to easily buy and sell (trade) financial securities (such as stocks and bonds), commodities (such as precious metals or agricultural goods), and other fungible items of value at low transaction costs and at prices that reflect the efficient-market hypothesis.

_____s have evolved significantly over several hundred years and are undergoing constant innovation to improve liquidity.

Both general markets (where many commodities are traded) and specialized markets (where only one commodity is traded) exist.
- a. Convertible arbitrage
- b. Noise trader
- c. Market anomaly
- d. Financial market

22. A _____, reserve bank, or monetary authority is the entity responsible for the monetary policy of a country or of a group of member states. It is a bank that can lend money to other banks in times of need. Its primary responsibility is to maintain the stability of the national currency and money supply, but more active duties include controlling subsidized-loan interest rates, and acting as a lender of last resort to the banking sector during times of financial crisis (private banks often being integral to the national financial system.)
- a. Central Bank
- b. 100-year flood
- c. 130-30 fund
- d. 1921 recession

23. The Bank of Russia or the _____ is the central bank of Russia. Its functions are described in the Russian constitution and in the special Federal law. Bank of Russia was founded on July 13, 1990, but traced its history to the State Bank of the Russian Empire.
- a. 130-30 fund
- b. 1921 recession
- c. 100-year flood
- d. Central Bank of the Russian Federation

24. _____ is a field of economics concerned with paying for collective or governmental activities, and with the administration and design of those activities. The field is often divided into questions of what the government or collective organizations should do or are doing, and questions of how to pay for those activities. The broader term (public economics) and the narrower term (government finance) are also often used.

a. Tax increment financing
c. Minimum Municipal Obligation
b. Value capture
d. Public finance

25. To _____ is to impose a financial charge or other levy upon a taxpayer by a state or the functional equivalent of a state.

_____es are also imposed by many subnational entities. _____es consist of direct _____ or indirect _____, and may be paid in money or as its labour equivalent (often but not always unpaid.)

a. 100-year flood
c. Tax
b. 1921 recession
d. 130-30 fund

26. To tax is to impose a financial charge or other levy upon a taxpayer by a state or the functional equivalent of a state.

_____ are also imposed by many subnational entities. _____ consist of direct tax or indirect tax, and may be paid in money or as its labour equivalent (often but not always unpaid.)

a. 1921 recession
c. 100-year flood
b. 130-30 fund
d. Taxes

27. The term _____ refers to government debt, expenditures and revenues, or to finance (particularly financial revenue) in general.

- _____ deficit is the budget deficit of federal or local government
- _____ policy is the discretionary spending of governments. Contrasts with monetary policy.
- _____ year and _____ quarter are reporting periods for firms and other agencies.

a. Procter ' Gamble
c. Bucket shop
b. Drawdown
d. Fiscal

28. The _____ , 1949-1991, was an economic organization of communist states and a kind of Eastern Bloc equivalent to--but more geographically inclusive than--the European Economic Community. The military equivalent to the Comecon was the Warsaw Pact, though Comecon's membership was significantly wider. The Comecon was the Eastern Bloc's reply to the formation of the OEEC .

a. 1921 recession
c. 130-30 fund
b. 100-year flood
d. Council for Mutual Economic Assistance

29. _____s is the social science that studies the production, distribution, and consumption of goods and services. The term _____s comes from the Ancient Greek oá¼°κονομῖα from oá¼¶κος (oikos, 'house') + vÍŒμος (nomos, 'custom' or 'law'), hence 'rules of the house(hold)'. Current _____ models developed out of the broader field of political economy in the late 19th century, owing to a desire to use an empirical approach more akin to the physical sciences.

a. Inflation
c. Economic
b. Energy economics
d. Opportunity cost

Chapter 8. The Russian Federation

30. _____ is money accepted for exchange of goods in an economy. The prevalence of one money over another arises, usually, when a government designates through decrees that the government shall accept only particular notes and coins in payment for taxes. Typically, money of _____ consists of stamped coins and minted paper bills.
   a. Security thread
   b. Totnes pound
   c. Local currency
   d. Currency

31. _____ is the shortage of common things such as food, clothing, shelter and safe drinking water, all of which determine the quality of life. It may also include the lack of access to opportunities such as education and employment which aid the escape from _____ and/or allow one to enjoy the respect of fellow citizens. According to Mollie Orshansky who developed the _____ measurements used by the U.S. government, 'to be poor is to be deprived of those goods and services and pleasures which others around us take for granted.' Ongoing debates over causes, effects and best ways to measure _____, directly influence the design and implementation of _____-reduction programs and are therefore relevant to the fields of public administration and international development.
   a. Poverty map
   b. Growth Elasticity of Poverty
   c. Poverty
   d. Liberal welfare reforms

32. The _____ is an international organization that oversees the global financial system by following the macroeconomic policies of its member countries, in particular those with an impact on exchange rates and the balance of payments. It is an organization formed to stabilize international exchange rates and facilitate development. It also offers financial and technical assistance to its members, making it an international lender of last resort.
   a. ACEA agreement
   b. ACCRA Cost of Living Index
   c. Office of Thrift Supervision
   d. International Monetary Fund

33. The _____ is an international financial institution that provides financial and technical assistance to developing countries for development programs (e.g. bridges, roads, schools, etc.) with the stated goal of reducing poverty.

The _____ differs from the _____ Group, in that the _____ comprises only two institutions:

- International Bank for Reconstruction and Development (IBRD)
- International Development Association (IDA)

Whereas the latter incorporates these two in addition to three more:

- International Finance Corporation (IFC)
- Multilateral Investment Guarantee Agency (MIGA)
- International Centre for Settlement of Investment Disputes (ICSID)

John Maynard Keynes (right) represented the UK at the conference, and Harry Dexter White represented the US.

The _____ is one of two major financial institutions created as a result of the Bretton Woods Conference in 1944. The International Monetary Fund, a related but separate institution, is the second.

   a. Bank-State-Branch
   b. Financial costs of the 2003 Iraq War
   c. Flow to Equity-Approach
   d. World Bank

34. The _____ is a trilateral trade bloc in North America created by the governments of the United States, Canada, and Mexico. The agreement creating the trade bloc came into force on January 1, 1994. It superseded the Canada-United States Free Trade Agreement between the U.S. and Canada.
   a. Demand-side technologies
   b. Federal Reserve Bank Notes
   c. Case-Shiller Home Price Indices
   d. North American Free Trade Agreement

35. _____ are usually numerical time-series, i.e., sets of data (covering periods of time) for part or all of a single economy or the international economy. When they are time-series the data sets are usually monthly but can be quarterly and annual. The data may be adjusted in various ways (for ease of further analysis), most commonly adjusted or unadjusted for seasonal fluctuations.
   a. ACEA agreement
   b. ACCRA Cost of Living Index
   c. AD-IA Model
   d. Economic data

Chapter 9. Poland, the Czech Republic, and Hungary

1. _____s is the social science that studies the production, distribution, and consumption of goods and services. The term _____s comes from the Ancient Greek οἰκονομία from οἶκος (oikos, 'house') + νόμος (nomos, 'custom' or 'law'), hence 'rules of the house(hold)'. Current _____ models developed out of the broader field of political economy in the late 19th century, owing to a desire to use an empirical approach more akin to the physical sciences.

   a. Economic
   b. Energy economics
   c. Inflation
   d. Opportunity cost

2. _____ refers to the actions that governments take in the economic field. It covers the systems for setting interest rates and government deficit as well as the labour market, national ownership, and many other areas of government.

   Such policies are often influenced by international institutions like the International Monetary Fund or World Bank as well as political beliefs and the consequent policies of parties.

   a. ACEA agreement
   b. ACCRA Cost of Living Index
   c. AD-IA Model
   d. Economic Policy

3. _____ was a German Communist politician who led the German Democratic Republic from 1971 until 1989.

   After German reunification, Honecker first fled to the Soviet Union but was extradited to Germany by the new Russian government. Back in Germany, he was imprisoned and tried for high treason and crimes committed during the Cold War.

   a. Erich Honecker
   b. Adam Smith
   c. Adolph Fischer
   d. Adolf Hitler

4. The _____ was an economic policy proposed by Vladimir Lenin to prevent the Russian economy from collapsing. Allowing some private ventures, the _____ allowed small businesses/shop for instant to reopen for private profit while the state continued to control banks, foreign trade, and large industries. It was officially decided in the course of the 10th Congress of the All-Russian Communist Party.

   a. Delancey Street Foundation
   b. Trade adjustment assistance
   c. Financial Crimes Enforcement Network
   d. New Economic Policy

5. _____ is a socioeconomic structure and political ideology that promotes the establishment of an egalitarian, classless, stateless society based on common ownership and control of the means of production and property in general. In political science, the term '_____' is sometimes used to refer to communist states, a form of government in which the state operates under a one-party system and declares allegiance to Marxism-Leninism or a derivative thereof, even if the party does not actually claim that it has already reached _____.

   Forerunners of communist ideas existed in antiquity and particularly in the 18th and early 19th century France, with thinkers such as Jean-Jacques Rousseau and the more radical Gracchus Babeuf.

   a. New Communist Movement
   b. Social fascism
   c. Democratic centralism
   d. Communism

Chapter 9. Poland, the Czech Republic, and Hungary

6. An _____ or Ă"conomic system is a system that involves the production, distribution and consumption of goods and services between the entities in a particular society. It is the method used by society to produce and distribute goods and services. The _____ is composed of people and institutions, including their relationships to productive resources, such as through the convention of property.
   a. Indicative planning
   b. Intention economy
   c. Information economy
   d. Economic system

7. The Communist Party of Peru, more commonly known as the _____ , is a Pseudo-Maoist guerrilla organization in Peru. When it first launched the internal conflict in Peru in 1980, its stated goal was to replace what it saw as bourgeois democracy with 'New Democracy.' The _____ believed that by imposing a dictatorship of the proletariat, inducing cultural revolution, and eventually sparking world revolution, they could arrive at pure communism. The _____ also believed that all existing socialist countries were revisionist, and that the _____ itself was the vanguard of the world communist movement.
   a. 130-30 fund
   b. Shining Path
   c. 1921 recession
   d. 100-year flood

8. _____ is the incidence or process of transferring ownership of a business, enterprise, agency or public service from the public sector (government) to the private sector (business.) In a broader sense, _____ refers to transfer of any government function to the private sector including governmental functions like revenue collection and law enforcement.

   The term '_____' also has been used to describe two unrelated transactions.

   a. Compound empowerment
   b. Ricardian equivalence
   c. Privatization
   d. Performance reports

9. _____ is a field of economics concerned with paying for collective or governmental activities, and with the administration and design of those activities. The field is often divided into questions of what the government or collective organizations should do or are doing, and questions of how to pay for those activities. The broader term (public economics) and the narrower term (government finance) are also often used.
   a. Minimum Municipal Obligation
   b. Value capture
   c. Tax increment financing
   d. Public finance

10. A _____ is a bond which is worth a certain monetary value and which may only be spent for specific reasons or on specific goods. Examples include -- but are not limited to -- housing, travel and food _____s. The term _____ is also a synonym for receipt, and is often used to refer to receipts used as evidence of, for example, the declaration that a service has been performed or that an expenditure has been made.
    a. 1921 recession
    b. 100-year flood
    c. Voucher
    d. 130-30 fund

11. The _____ was one of the peace treaties at the end of World War I. It ended the state of war between Germany and the Allied Powers. It was signed on 28 June 1919, exactly five years after the assassination of Archduke Franz Ferdinand. The other Central Powers on the German side of World War I were dealt with in separate treaties.
    a. 100-year flood
    b. Treaty of Versailles
    c. 1921 recession
    d. 130-30 fund

12. The _____ was a major economic reform launched in the People's Republic of Hungary in 1968.

The period from 1956-1968 was one of reform in Eastern Europe. The beginning of these transformations was marked by the Hungarian Revolution of 1956 which resulted in János Kádár's placement as the communist leader of the People's Republic of Hungary and the creation of the Hungarian Socialist Workers' Party (HSWP.)

a. New Economic Mechanism
b. 1921 recession
c. 130-30 fund
d. 100-year flood

13. The _____ is a medium-sized, structurally, politically, and institutionally open economy in Central Europe and is part of the EU single market. Like most Eastern European economies, it experienced market liberalisation in the early 1990s as part of a transition away from communism. Today, Hungary is a full member of OECD and the World Trade Organization.

a. 1921 recession
b. Hungarian economy
c. 130-30 fund
d. 100-year flood

14. _____ in economics refers to metrics and measures of output from production processes, per unit of input. Labor _____, for example, is typically measured as a ratio of output per labor-hour, an input. _____ may be conceived of as a metrics of the technical or engineering efficiency of production.

a. Production-possibility frontier
b. Piece work
c. Fordism
d. Productivity

Chapter 10. Problems of the Less Developed Countries

1. _____ is a socioeconomic structure and political ideology that promotes the establishment of an egalitarian, classless, stateless society based on common ownership and control of the means of production and property in general. In political science, the term '_____' is sometimes used to refer to communist states, a form of government in which the state operates under a one-party system and declares allegiance to Marxism-Leninism or a derivative thereof, even if the party does not actually claim that it has already reached _____.

Forerunners of communist ideas existed in antiquity and particularly in the 18th and early 19th century France, with thinkers such as Jean-Jacques Rousseau and the more radical Gracchus Babeuf.

    a. Communism   b. Social fascism
    c. New Communist Movement   d. Democratic centralism

2. _____s is the social science that studies the production, distribution, and consumption of goods and services. The term _____s comes from the Ancient Greek οἰκονομία from οἶκος (oikos, 'house') + νόμος (nomos, 'custom' or 'law'), hence 'rules of the house(hold)'. Current _____ models developed out of the broader field of political economy in the late 19th century, owing to a desire to use an empirical approach more akin to the physical sciences.

    a. Inflation   b. Economic
    c. Opportunity cost   d. Energy economics

3. _____ is the development of economic wealth of countries or regions for the well-being of their inhabitants. It is the process by which a nation improves the economic, political, and social well being of its people. From a policy perspective, _____ can be defined as efforts that seek to improve the economic well-being and quality of life for a community by creating and/or retaining jobs and supporting or growing incomes and the tax base.

    a. Economic methodology   b. Experimental economics
    c. Economic development   d. Inflation

4. _____ is the increase in the amount of the goods and services produced by an economy over time. It is conventionally measured as the percent rate of increase in real gross domestic product, or real GDP. Growth is usually calculated in real terms, i.e. inflation-adjusted terms, in order to net out the effect of inflation on the price of the goods and services produced.

    a. AD-IA Model   b. ACEA agreement
    c. Economic growth   d. ACCRA Cost of Living Index

Chapter 10. Problems of the Less Developed Countries

5. _____ has several particular meanings:

   - in mathematics
     - _____ function
     - Euler _____
     - _____
     - _____ subgroup
     - method of _____s (partial differential equations)
   - in physics and engineering
     - any _____ curve that shows the relationship between certain input- and output parameters, e.g.
     - an I-V or current-voltage _____ is the current in a circuit as a function of the applied voltage
     - Receiver-Operator _____
   - in fiction
     - in Dungeons ' Dragons, _____ is another name for ability score

   a. Russian financial crisis
   b. Demand
   c. Technocracy
   d. Characteristic

6. _____ is a misspelled phrase from Latin 'pro capite' phrase meaning per head with pro meaning 'per' or 'for each' and capite meaning 'head.' Both words together equate to the phrase 'for each head.'

It is usually used in the field of statistics to indicate the average per person for any given concern, such as income, crime rate, etc.

It is also used in wills to indicate that each of the named beneficiaries should receive, by devise or bequest, equal shares of the estate. This is in contrast to a per stirpes division, in which each branch of the inheriting family inherits an equal share of the estate.

   a. Per capita
   b. False positive rate
   c. Sargan test
   d. Population statistics

7. _____ means how much each individual receives, in monetary terms, of the yearly income generated in the country. This is what each citizen is to receive if the yearly national income is divided equally among everyone. _____ is usually reported in units of currency per year.
   a. Per capita income
   b. Real income
   c. Family income
   d. Lerman ratio

8. _____ is the shortage of common things such as food, clothing, shelter and safe drinking water, all of which determine the quality of life. It may also include the lack of access to opportunities such as education and employment which aid the escape from _____ and/or allow one to enjoy the respect of fellow citizens. According to Mollie Orshansky who developed the _____ measurements used by the U.S. government, 'to be poor is to be deprived of those goods and services and pleasures which others around us take for granted.' Ongoing debates over causes, effects and best ways to measure _____, directly influence the design and implementation of _____-reduction programs and are therefore relevant to the fields of public administration and international development.

Chapter 10. Problems of the Less Developed Countries

a. Poverty
b. Liberal welfare reforms
c. Growth Elasticity of Poverty
d. Poverty map

9. The traditional definition of _____ is considered to be the ability to use language to read, write, listen, and speak. In modern contexts, the word refers to reading and writing at a level adequate for communication, or at a level that lets one understand and communicate ideas in a literate society, so as to take part in that society. The United Nations Educational, Scientific and Cultural Organization (UNESCO) has drafted the following definition: "_____' is the ability to identify, understand, interpret, create, communicate, compute and use printed and written materials associated with varying contexts.
a. 100-year flood
b. 130-30 fund
c. 1921 recession
d. Literacy

10. _____ was a German Communist politician who led the German Democratic Republic from 1971 until 1989.

After German reunification, Honecker first fled to the Soviet Union but was extradited to Germany by the new Russian government. Back in Germany, he was imprisoned and tried for high treason and crimes committed during the Cold War.

a. Adolph Fischer
b. Adam Smith
c. Adolf Hitler
d. Erich Honecker

11. The _____ is an index used to rank countries by level of 'human development', which usually also implies whether a country is a developed, developing, or underdeveloped country.

The _____ combines normalized measures of life expectancy, literacy, educational attainment, and GDP per capita for countries worldwide. It is claimed as a standard means of measuring human development--a concept that, according to the United Nations Development Program (UNDP), refers to the process of widening the options of persons, giving them greater opportunities for education, health care, income, employment, etc.

a. 1921 recession
b. Human Development Index
c. 100-year flood
d. 130-30 fund

12. The _____ is a trilateral trade bloc in North America created by the governments of the United States, Canada, and Mexico. The agreement creating the trade bloc came into force on January 1, 1994. It superseded the Canada-United States Free Trade Agreement between the U.S. and Canada.
a. Demand-side technologies
b. North American Free Trade Agreement
c. Case-Shiller Home Price Indices
d. Federal Reserve Bank Notes

13. In economics, the people in the _____ are the suppliers of labor. The _____ is all the nonmilitary people who are employed or unemployed. In 2005, the worldwide _____ was over 3 billion people.
a. Departmentalization
b. Labor force
c. Grenelle agreements
d. Distributed workforce

14. _____ is the change in population over time, and can be quantified as the change in the number of individuals in a population using 'per unit time' for measurement. The term _____ can technically refer to any species, but almost always refers to humans, and it is often used informally for the more specific demographic term _____ rate , and is often used to refer specifically to the growth of the population of the world.

Chapter 10. Problems of the Less Developed Countries

Simple models of _____ include the Malthusian Growth Model and the logistic model.

a. 100-year flood
c. 130-30 fund
b. Population dynamics
d. Population growth

15. The term '_____' refers to the concept of collecting information and attempting to spot a pattern in the information. In some fields of study, the term '_____' has more formally-defined meanings.

In project management _____ is a mathematical technique that uses historical results to predict future outcome.

a. Probit model
c. Coefficient of determination
b. Trend analysis
d. Quantile regression

16. _____ is the physical growth of rural or natural land into urban areas as a result of population immigration to an existing urban area. Effects include change in density and administration services. While the exact definition and population size of urbanized areas varies among different countries, _____ is attributed to growth of cities.

a. Urban prairie
c. ACCRA Cost of Living Index
b. Urban renewal
d. Urbanization

17. _____ Abd al-Majid al-Tikriti was the President of Iraq from July 16, 1979 until April 9, 2003.

A leading member of the revolutionary Ba'ath Party, which espoused secular pan-Arabism, economic modernization, and Arab socialism, Saddam played a key role in the 1968 coup that brought the party to long-term power. As vice president under the ailing General Ahmed Hassan al-Bakr, Saddam tightly controlled conflict between the government and the armed forces--at a time when many other groups were considered capable of overthrowing the government--by creating repressive security forces.

a. Adolph Fischer
c. Adam Smith
b. Adolf Hitler
d. Saddam Hussein

18. In economics, an _____ is any good or commodity, transported from one country to another country in a legitimate fashion, typically for use in trade. _____ goods or services are provided to foreign consumers by domestic producers. _____ is an important part of international trade.

a. ACCRA Cost of Living Index
c. AD-IA Model
b. ACEA agreement
d. Export

19. _____ is that which is owed; usually referencing assets owed, but the term can also cover moral obligations and other interactions not requiring money. In the case of assets, _____ is a means of using future purchasing power in the present before a summation has been earned. Some companies and corporations use _____ as a part of their overall corporate finance strategy.

a. Collateral Management
c. Debt
b. Hard money loan
d. Debenture

Chapter 10. Problems of the Less Developed Countries

20. _____ is that part of the total debt in a country that is owed to creditors outside the country. The debtors can be the government, corporations or private households. The debt includes money owed to private commercial banks, other governments, or international financial institutions such as the IMF and World Bank.
   a. Asset protection
   b. Internal debt
   c. International debt collection
   d. External debt

21. _____ was a prominent Chinese politician. As leader of the Communist Party of China, Deng became a reformer who led China towards market economics. While Deng never held office as the head of state or the head of government, he nonetheless served as the Paramount leader of the People's Republic of China from 1978 to the early 1990s.
   a. Adolf Hitler
   b. Adam Smith
   c. Adolph Fischer
   d. Deng Xiaoping

22. A _____ is the procedure of systematically acquiring and recording information about the members of a given population. It is a regularly occurring and official count of a particular population. The term is used mostly in connection with national 'population and door to door _____es' (to be taken every 10 years according to United Nations recommendations), agriculture, and business _____es.
   a. 1921 recession
   b. Census
   c. 100-year flood
   d. 130-30 fund

23. The Organisation for Economic Co-operation and Development (_____) is an international organisation of 30 countries that accept the principles of representative democracy and free-market economy. Most _____ members are high-income economies with a high HDI and are regarded as developed countries.

    It originated in 1948 as the Organisation for European Economic Co-operation, led by Robert Marjolin of France, to help administer the Marshall Plan for the reconstruction of Europe after World War II.

   a. ACCRA Cost of Living Index
   b. OECD
   c. AD-IA Model
   d. ACEA agreement

24. _____ is any process which seeks to reduce the level of poverty in a community, or amongst a group of people or countries. _____ programs may be aimed at economic or non-economic poverty. Some of the popular methods used are education, economic development, and income redistribution.
   a. Primary poverty
   b. Poverty reduction
   c. Poverty map
   d. Secondary poverty

Chapter 11. China

1. The _____ is an index used to rank countries by level of 'human development', which usually also implies whether a country is a developed, developing, or underdeveloped country.

The _____ combines normalized measures of life expectancy, literacy, educational attainment, and GDP per capita for countries worldwide. It is claimed as a standard means of measuring human development--a concept that, according to the United Nations Development Program (UNDP), refers to the process of widening the options of persons, giving them greater opportunities for education, health care, income, employment, etc.

   a. 1921 recession
   b. 100-year flood
   c. 130-30 fund
   d. Human Development Index

2. The _____ is an international financial institution that provides financial and technical assistance to developing countries for development programs (e.g. bridges, roads, schools, etc.) with the stated goal of reducing poverty.

The _____ differs from the _____ Group, in that the _____ comprises only two institutions:

- International Bank for Reconstruction and Development (IBRD)
- International Development Association (IDA)

Whereas the latter incorporates these two in addition to three more:

- International Finance Corporation (IFC)
- Multilateral Investment Guarantee Agency (MIGA)
- International Centre for Settlement of Investment Disputes (ICSID)

John Maynard Keynes (right) represented the UK at the conference, and Harry Dexter White represented the US.

The _____ is one of two major financial institutions created as a result of the Bretton Woods Conference in 1944. The International Monetary Fund, a related but separate institution, is the second.

   a. Bank-State-Branch
   b. Flow to Equity-Approach
   c. Financial costs of the 2003 Iraq War
   d. World Bank

3. _____s is the social science that studies the production, distribution, and consumption of goods and services. The term _____s comes from the Ancient Greek oá¼°κονομῖα from oá¼¶κος (oikos, 'house') + vÏŒμος (nomos, 'custom' or 'law'), hence 'rules of the house(hold)'. Current _____ models developed out of the broader field of political economy in the late 19th century, owing to a desire to use an empirical approach more akin to the physical sciences.
   a. Inflation
   b. Opportunity cost
   c. Economic
   d. Energy economics

4. _____ are usually numerical time-series, i.e., sets of data (covering periods of time) for part or all of a single economy or the international economy. When they are time-series the data sets are usually monthly but can be quarterly and annual. The data may be adjusted in various ways (for ease of further analysis), most commonly adjusted or unadjusted for seasonal fluctuations.

a. ACEA agreement
b. Economic data
c. AD-IA Model
d. ACCRA Cost of Living Index

5. The _____ of the USSR was a list of economic goals that was designed to strengthen the country's economy between 1928 and 1932, making the nation both militarily and industrially self-sufficient. 'We are fifty or a hundred years behind the advanced countries. We must make good this distance in ten years.

a. 130-30 fund
b. 1921 recession
c. 100-year flood
d. First Five-Year Plan

6. An _____ or Å"conomic system is a system that involves the production, distribution and consumption of goods and services between the entities in a particular society. It is the method used by society to produce and distribute goods and services. The _____ is composed of people and institutions, including their relationships to productive resources, such as through the convention of property.

a. Intention economy
b. Economic system
c. Information economy
d. Indicative planning

7. The _____ of the People's Republic of China was an economic and social plan used from 1958 to 1961 which aimed to use China's vast population to rapidly transform China from a primarily agrarian economy by peasant farmers into a modern communist society through the process of agriculturalization and industrialization. Mao Zedong based this program on the Theory of Productive Forces. It ended in catastrophe as it triggered a widespread famine that resulted in millions of premature deaths.

a. Global citizens movement
b. Deutsche Bank
c. Mittelstand
d. Great Leap Forward

8. The Great Proletarian _____ in the People's Republic of China was a period of widespread social and political upheaval; the nation-wide chaos and economic disarray engulfed much of Chinese society between 1966 and 1976.

It was launched by Mao Zedong, the chairman of the Communist Party of China, on May 16, 1966, who alleged that liberal bourgeoisie elements were dominating the party and insisted that they needed to be removed through post-revolutionary class struggle by mobilizing the thoughts and actions of China's youth, who formed Red Guards groups around the country. Although Mao himself officially declared the _____ to have ended in 1969, today it is widely believed that the power struggles and political instability between 1969 and the arrest of the Gang of Four as well as the death of Mao in 1976 were also part of the Revolution.

a. 100-year flood
b. 130-30 fund
c. 1921 recession
d. Cultural Revolution

9. _____ was the first Premier of the People's Republic of China, serving from October 1949 until his death in January 1976. Zhou was instrumental in the Communist Party's rise to power, and subsequently in the development of the Chinese Communist economy and restructuring of Chinese society.

A skilled and able diplomat, Zhou served as the Chinese foreign minister from 1949 to 1958.

a. Adolf Hitler
b. Adam Smith
c. Adolph Fischer
d. Zhou En-lai

10. _____ was a prominent Chinese politician. As leader of the Communist Party of China, Deng became a reformer who led China towards market economics. While Deng never held office as the head of state or the head of government, he nonetheless served as the Paramount leader of the People's Republic of China from 1978 to the early 1990s.
   a. Adam Smith
   b. Adolph Fischer
   c. Adolf Hitler
   d. Deng Xiaoping

11. A political party described as a _____ includes those that advocate the application of the social principles of communism through a communist form of government. The name originates from the 1848 tract Manifesto of the _____ by Karl Marx, Friedrich Engels. The Leninist concept of a _____ encompasses a larger political system and includes not only an ideological orientation but also a wide set of organizational policies.
   a. Criticisms of Communist party rule
   b. Criticisms of anarcho-capitalism
   c. Communism
   d. Communist Party

12. _____ is a type of trade policy that allows traders to act and transact without interference from government. Thus, the policy permits trading partners mutual gains from trade, with goods and services produced according to the theory of comparative advantage.

Under a _____ policy, prices are a reflection of true supply and demand, and are the sole determinant of resource allocation.

   a. 1921 recession
   b. Free Trade
   c. 130-30 fund
   d. 100-year flood

13. The _____ is a trilateral trade bloc in North America created by the governments of the United States, Canada, and Mexico. The agreement creating the trade bloc came into force on January 1, 1994. It superseded the Canada-United States Free Trade Agreement between the U.S. and Canada.
   a. Federal Reserve Bank Notes
   b. Demand-side technologies
   c. Case-Shiller Home Price Indices
   d. North American Free Trade Agreement

14. Economic interventionism or _____ is an action in a Market economy taken by a government, beyond the basic regulation of fraud and enforcement of contracts, in an effort to affect its own economy. Economic intervention can be aimed at a variety of political or economic objectives, such as promoting economic growth, increasing employment, raising wages, raising or reducing prices, promoting equality, managing the money supply and interest rates, increasing profits, or addressing market failures. The intervention may to direct, or indirect as in the case of indicative planning.
   a. ACEA agreement
   b. AD-IA Model
   c. ACCRA Cost of Living Index
   d. Economic planning

15. _____ is a movement within Christianity that originated in the sixteenth-century Protestant Reformation. It is considered to be one of the principal traditions within Christianity, together with Roman Catholicism and Eastern Orthodoxy. Anglicanism and Nontrinitarian Christianity, both of which are significantly influenced by _____, are also sometimes considered separate traditions.
   a. 130-30 fund
   b. 1921 recession
   c. 100-year flood
   d. Protestantism

16. _____ is a field of economics concerned with paying for collective or governmental activities, and with the administration and design of those activities. The field is often divided into questions of what the government or collective organizations should do or are doing, and questions of how to pay for those activities. The broader term (public economics) and the narrower term (government finance) are also often used.
   a. Tax increment financing
   b. Value capture
   c. Minimum Municipal Obligation
   d. Public finance

17. The _____ was a period in the late 18th and early 19th centuries when major changes in agriculture, manufacturing, mining, and transportation had a profound effect on the socioeconomic and cultural conditions in Britain. The changes subsequently spread throughout Europe, North America, and eventually the world. The onset of the _____ marked a major turning point in human society; almost every aspect of daily life was eventually influenced in some way.
   a. Adolf Hitler
   b. Adolph Fischer
   c. Adam Smith
   d. Industrial Revolution

18. A security is a fungible, negotiable instrument representing financial value. _____ are broadly categorized into debt _____; equity _____, e.g., common stocks; and derivative (finance) contracts such as forwards, futures, options and swaps. The company or other entity issuing the security is called the issuer.
   a. Settlement risk
   b. Red herring prospectus
   c. Pass-Through Certificates
   d. Securities

19. A _____ is a group of people who share or are motivated by at least one common issue or interest, or work together on a specific project(s) to achieve a common objective. _____s are also characterised by attempts to share and exercise political and social power and to make decisions on a consensus-driven and egalitarian basis. _____s differ from cooperatives in that they are not necessarily focused upon an economic benefit or saving (but can be that as well.)
   a. 130-30 fund
   b. 1921 recession
   c. 100-year flood
   d. Collective

20. A _____, state-owned enterprise or government business enterprise is a legal entity created by a government to undertake commercial or business activities on behalf of an owner government. There is no standard definition of a _____ or state-owned enterprise (SOE), although the two terms can be used inter-changeably. The defining characteristics are that they have a distinct legal form and they are established to operate in commercial affairs.
   a. Luxembourg Income Study
   b. Citizens for an Alternative Tax System
   c. Government-owned corporation
   d. Non-governmental organization

21. A _____ is an entity formed between two or more parties to undertake economic activity together. The parties agree to create a new entity by both contributing equity, and they then share in the revenues, expenses, and control of the enterprise. The venture can be for one specific project only, or a continuing business relationship such as the Fuji Xerox _____.
   a. Nexus of contracts
   b. Joint venture
   c. Property right
   d. Business valuation

22. An _____ is a person who has possession of an enterprise and assumes significant accountability for the inherent risks and the outcome. It is an ambitious leader who combines land, labor, and capital to create and market new goods or services. The term is a loanword from French and was first defined by the Irish economist Richard Cantillon.

a. ACCRA Cost of Living Index	b. ACEA agreement
c. Expansionary policies	d. Entrepreneur

23. Under the system of feudalism, a _____, fief, feud, feoff often consisted of inheritable lands or revenue-producing property granted by a liege lord, generally to a vassal, in return for a form of allegiance, originally to give him the means to fulfill his military duties when called upon. However anything of value could be held in fief, such as an office, a right of exploitation (e.g., hunting, fishing) or any other type of revenue, rather than the land it comes from.

Originally, the feudal institution of vassalage did not imply the giving or receiving of landholdings (which were granted only as a reward for loyalty), but by the eighth century the giving of a landholding was becoming standard.

a. 130-30 fund	b. 100-year flood
c. 1921 recession	d. Fiefdom

24. The _____ lasted from 1839 to 1842 and 1856 to 1860, the climax of a trade dispute between China under the Qing Dynasty and the British Empire. British smuggling of opium from British India into China in defiance of China's drug laws erupted into open warfare between Britain and China.

China was defeated in both wars leaving its government having to tolerate the opium trade.

a. ACCRA Cost of Living Index	b. Opium Wars
c. AD-IA Model	d. ACEA agreement

Chapter 12. India

1. The _____ is an international financial institution that provides financial and technical assistance to developing countries for development programs (e.g. bridges, roads, schools, etc.) with the stated goal of reducing poverty.

The _____ differs from the _____ Group, in that the _____ comprises only two institutions:

- International Bank for Reconstruction and Development (IBRD)
- International Development Association (IDA)

Whereas the latter incorporates these two in addition to three more:

- International Finance Corporation (IFC)
- Multilateral Investment Guarantee Agency (MIGA)
- International Centre for Settlement of Investment Disputes (ICSID)

John Maynard Keynes (right) represented the UK at the conference, and Harry Dexter White represented the US.

The _____ is one of two major financial institutions created as a result of the Bretton Woods Conference in 1944. The International Monetary Fund, a related but separate institution, is the second.

a. World Bank
b. Financial costs of the 2003 Iraq War
c. Bank-State-Branch
d. Flow to Equity-Approach

2. _____s is the social science that studies the production, distribution, and consumption of goods and services. The term _____s comes from the Ancient Greek oá¼°κονομῖα from oá¼¶κος (oikos, 'house') + vίŒμος (nomos, 'custom' or 'law'), hence 'rules of the house(hold)'. Current _____ models developed out of the broader field of political economy in the late 19th century, owing to a desire to use an empirical approach more akin to the physical sciences.
a. Inflation
b. Energy economics
c. Opportunity cost
d. Economic

3. _____ are usually numerical time-series, i.e., sets of data (covering periods of time) for part or all of a single economy or the international economy. When they are time-series the data sets are usually monthly but can be quarterly and annual. The data may be adjusted in various ways (for ease of further analysis), most commonly adjusted or unadjusted for seasonal fluctuations.
a. Economic data
b. AD-IA Model
c. ACCRA Cost of Living Index
d. ACEA agreement

4. _____ is an economic theory that holds that the prosperity of a nation is dependent upon its supply of capital, and that the global volume of international trade is 'unchangeable.' Economic assets or capital, are represented by bullion (gold, silver, and trade value) held by the state, which is best increased through a positive balance of trade with other nations (exports minus imports.) _____ suggests that the ruling government should advance these goals by playing a protectionist role in the economy; by encouraging exports and discouraging imports, notably through the use of tariffs and subsidies.

_____ was the dominant school of thought throughout the early modern period (from the 16th to the 18th century.)

a. Consumer theory
b. Mercantilism
c. Nominal value
d. General equilibrium theory

5. The _____ was an early English joint-stock company that was formed initially for pursuing trade with the East Indies, but that ended up trading with the Indian subcontinent and China. The oldest among several similarly formed European East India Companies, the Company was granted an English Royal Charter, under the name Governor and Company of Merchants of London Trading into the East Indies, by Elizabeth I on 31 December 1600. After a rival English company challenged its monopoly in the late 17th century, the two companies were merged in 1708 to form the United Company of Merchants of England Trading to the East Indies, commonly styled the Honourable _____, and abbreviated, HEast India Company; the Company was colloquially referred to as John Company, and in India as Company Bahadur.
   a. AD-IA Model
   b. ACEA agreement
   c. ACCRA Cost of Living Index
   d. East India Company

6. _____ is the development of economic wealth of countries or regions for the well-being of their inhabitants. It is the process by which a nation improves the economic, political, and social well being of its people. From a policy perspective, _____ can be defined as efforts that seek to improve the economic well-being and quality of life for a community by creating and/or retaining jobs and supporting or growing incomes and the tax base.
   a. Economic development
   b. Economic methodology
   c. Experimental economics
   d. Inflation

7. The term _____ incorporates various national and regional campaigns, agitations and efforts of both Nonviolent and Militant philosophy. The term encompasses a wide spectrum of political organizations, philosophies, and movements which had the common aim of ending the British Colonial Authority as well as other colonial administrations in South Asia. The initial resistance to the movement can be traced back to the very beginnings of Colonial Expansion in Karnataka by the Portuguese in the 16th century and by the British East India Company in Bengal, in the middle and late 1700s.
   a. Indian national movement
   b. Adolf Hitler
   c. Adam Smith
   d. Adolph Fischer

8. _____ was the first, and has been the longest-serving prime minister of India so far, having served from 1947 to 1964. A leading figure in the Indian independence movement, Nehru was elected by the Congress party to assume office as independent India's first Prime Minister, and later when the Congress won India's first general election in 1952. As one of the founders of the Non-aligned Movement, he was also an important figure in the international politics of the post-war era.
   a. Adam Smith
   b. Adolf Hitler
   c. Adolph Fischer
   d. Jawaharlal Nehru

9. _____ is the structure and set of regulations in place to control activity, usually in large organizations and government. As opposed to adhocracy, it is represented by standardized procedure (rule-following) that dictates the execution of most or all processes within the body, formal division of powers, hierarchy, and relationships. In practice the interpretation and execution of policy can lead to informal influence.
   a. 1921 recession
   b. 130-30 fund
   c. 100-year flood
   d. Bureaucracy

Chapter 12. India

10. Economic interventionism or _____ is an action in a Market economy taken by a government, beyond the basic regulation of fraud and enforcement of contracts, in an effort to affect its own economy. Economic intervention can be aimed at a variety of political or economic objectives, such as promoting economic growth, increasing employment, raising wages, raising or reducing prices, promoting equality, managing the money supply and interest rates, increasing profits, or addressing market failures. The intervention may to direct, or indirect as in the case of indicative planning.
    a. AD-IA Model
    b. Economic planning
    c. ACCRA Cost of Living Index
    d. ACEA agreement

11. _____ is the act of taking an industry or assets into the public ownership of a national government or state. _____ usually refers to private assets, but may also mean assets owned by lower levels of government, such as municipalities, being state operated or owned by the state. The opposite of _____ is usually privatization or de-nationalisation, but may also be municipalization.
    a. Nationalization
    b. Social discount rate
    c. Privileged group
    d. Ricardian equivalence

12. _____ is a measure of the strength of a brand, product, service relative to competitive offerings. There is often a geographic element to the competitive landscape. In defining _____, you must see to what extent a product, brand, or firm controls a product category in a given geographic area.
    a. Demand shaping
    b. Market dominance
    c. Price elasticity of supply
    d. Horizontal territorial allocation

13. _____ was the Prime Minister of the Republic of India for three consecutive terms from 1966 to 1977 and for a fourth term from 1980 until her assassination in 1984, a total of fifteen years. She was India's first and, to date, only female Prime Minister.

Born in the politically influential Nehru Family, she grew up in an intensely political atmosphere.

    a. Adolf Hitler
    b. Indira Priyadarshini Gandhi
    c. Adam Smith
    d. Adolph Fischer

14. The _____ is an international organization that oversees the global financial system by following the macroeconomic policies of its member countries, in particular those with an impact on exchange rates and the balance of payments. It is an organization formed to stabilize international exchange rates and facilitate development. It also offers financial and technical assistance to its members, making it an international lender of last resort.
    a. ACCRA Cost of Living Index
    b. ACEA agreement
    c. Office of Thrift Supervision
    d. International Monetary Fund

15. To _____ is to impose a financial charge or other levy upon a taxpayer by a state or the functional equivalent of a state.

_____es are also imposed by many subnational entities. _____es consist of direct _____ or indirect _____, and may be paid in money or as its labour equivalent (often but not always unpaid.)

    a. 1921 recession
    b. Tax
    c. 100-year flood
    d. 130-30 fund

16. _____ is the process of changing the way taxes are collected or managed by the government.

_____ers have different goals. Some seek to reduce the level of taxation of all people by the government.

a. Nil-rate band
b. Special-purpose local-option sales tax
c. Tax break
d. Tax reform

17. To tax is to impose a financial charge or other levy upon a taxpayer by a state or the functional equivalent of a state.

_____ are also imposed by many subnational entities. _____ consist of direct tax or indirect tax, and may be paid in money or as its labour equivalent (often but not always unpaid.)

a. 1921 recession
b. 130-30 fund
c. 100-year flood
d. Taxes

18. The _____ is an index used to rank countries by level of 'human development', which usually also implies whether a country is a developed, developing, or underdeveloped country.

The _____ combines normalized measures of life expectancy, literacy, educational attainment, and GDP per capita for countries worldwide. It is claimed as a standard means of measuring human development--a concept that, according to the United Nations Development Program (UNDP), refers to the process of widening the options of persons, giving them greater opportunities for education, health care, income, employment, etc.

a. 100-year flood
b. 1921 recession
c. 130-30 fund
d. Human Development Index

Chapter 13. Latin America: Argentina, Brazil, and Mexico

1. _____ is an economic theory that holds that the prosperity of a nation is dependent upon its supply of capital, and that the global volume of international trade is 'unchangeable.' Economic assets or capital, are represented by bullion (gold, silver, and trade value) held by the state, which is best increased through a positive balance of trade with other nations (exports minus imports.) _____ suggests that the ruling government should advance these goals by playing a protectionist role in the economy; by encouraging exports and discouraging imports, notably through the use of tariffs and subsidies.

_____ was the dominant school of thought throughout the early modern period (from the 16th to the 18th century.)

   a. General equilibrium theory
   c. Nominal value
   b. Consumer theory
   d. Mercantilism

2. The _____ was an early English joint-stock company that was formed initially for pursuing trade with the East Indies, but that ended up trading with the Indian subcontinent and China. The oldest among several similarly formed European East India Companies, the Company was granted an English Royal Charter, under the name Governor and Company of Merchants of London Trading into the East Indies, by Elizabeth I on 31 December 1600. After a rival English company challenged its monopoly in the late 17th century, the two companies were merged in 1708 to form the United Company of Merchants of England Trading to the East Indies, commonly styled the Honourable _____, and abbreviated, HEast India Company; the Company was colloquially referred to as John Company, and in India as Company Bahadur.
   a. ACEA agreement
   c. ACCRA Cost of Living Index
   b. AD-IA Model
   d. East India Company

3. The _____ was a trading company, which was established in 1602, when the States-General of the Netherlands granted it a 21-year monopoly to carry out colonial activities in Asia. It was the first multinational corporation in the world and the first company to issue stock. It was also arguably the world's first megacorporation, possessing quasi-governmental powers, including the ability to wage war, negotiate treaties, coin money, and establish colonies.
   a. 1921 recession
   c. 100-year flood
   b. Dutch East India Company
   d. 130-30 fund

4. _____ is a type of trade policy that allows traders to act and transact without interference from government. Thus, the policy permits trading partners mutual gains from trade, with goods and services produced according to the theory of comparative advantage.

Under a _____ policy, prices are a reflection of true supply and demand, and are the sole determinant of resource allocation.

   a. 130-30 fund
   c. Free trade
   b. 100-year flood
   d. 1921 recession

5. A _____ is crossing the border without being taxed for it.

A _____ or export processing zone (EPZ) is one or more special areas of a country where some normal trade barriers such as tariffs and quotas are eliminated and bureaucratic requirements are lowered in hopes of attracting new business and foreign investments. It is a a region where a group of countries has agreed to reduce or eliminate trade barriers.

Chapter 13. Latin America: Argentina, Brazil, and Mexico

a. Free trade zone
b. Competitiveness
c. Heckscher-Ohlin model
d. Most favoured nation

6. In economics, _____ is a rise in the general level of prices of goods and services in an economy over a period of time. When the general price level rises, each unit of currency buys fewer goods and services; consequently, _____ is also a decline in the real value of money--a loss of purchasing power in the medium of exchange which is also the monetary unit of account in the economy. A chief measure of general price-level _____ is the general _____ rate, which is the percentage change in a general price index (normally the Consumer Price Index) over time.
   a. Opportunity cost
   b. Energy economics
   c. Economic
   d. Inflation

7. The _____ is a United Nations initiative to grant self-determination to Western Sahara. It was intended to replace the Settlement Plan of 1991, which was further detailed in the Houston Agreement of 1997.

Western Sahara's administration by Morocco since 1975 is challenged by Polisario guerillas living in exile in neighbouring Algeria.

   a. 1921 recession
   b. 100-year flood
   c. 130-30 fund
   d. Baker Plan

8. The _____ , 1949-1991, was an economic organization of communist states and a kind of Eastern Bloc equivalent to--but more geographically inclusive than--the European Economic Community. The military equivalent to the Comecon was the Warsaw Pact, though Comecon's membership was significantly wider. The Comecon was the Eastern Bloc's reply to the formation of the OEEC .
   a. 1921 recession
   b. Council for Mutual Economic Assistance
   c. 100-year flood
   d. 130-30 fund

9. _____s is the social science that studies the production, distribution, and consumption of goods and services. The term _____s comes from the Ancient Greek oá¼°κονομῖα from oá¼¶κος (oikos, 'house') + vΌμος (nomos, 'custom' or 'law'), hence 'rules of the house(hold)'. Current _____ models developed out of the broader field of political economy in the late 19th century, owing to a desire to use an empirical approach more akin to the physical sciences.
   a. Economic
   b. Inflation
   c. Opportunity cost
   d. Energy economics

10. The _____ is an international organization that oversees the global financial system by following the macroeconomic policies of its member countries, in particular those with an impact on exchange rates and the balance of payments. It is an organization formed to stabilize international exchange rates and facilitate development. It also offers financial and technical assistance to its members, making it an international lender of last resort.
    a. ACCRA Cost of Living Index
    b. ACEA agreement
    c. Office of Thrift Supervision
    d. International Monetary Fund

11. _____ is that which is owed; usually referencing assets owed, but the term can also cover moral obligations and other interactions not requiring money. In the case of assets, _____ is a means of using future purchasing power in the present before a summation has been earned. Some companies and corporations use _____ as a part of their overall corporate finance strategy.

Chapter 13. Latin America: Argentina, Brazil, and Mexico

a. Debenture
b. Collateral Management
c. Hard money loan
d. Debt

12. _____ is that part of the total debt in a country that is owed to creditors outside the country. The debtors can be the government, corporations or private households. The debt includes money owed to private commercial banks, other governments, or international financial institutions such as the IMF and World Bank.
   a. International debt collection
   b. Asset protection
   c. External debt
   d. Internal debt

13. The _____ is a measure of statistical dispersion, commonly used as a measure of inequality of income distribution or inequality of wealth distribution. It is defined as a ratio with values between 0 and 1: A low _____ indicates more equal income or wealth distribution, while a high _____ indicates more unequal distribution. 0 corresponds to perfect equality (everyone having exactly the same income) and 1 corresponds to perfect inequality (where one person has all the income, while everyone else has zero income.)
   a. Suits index
   b. Compensating variation
   c. Gini coefficient
   d. Leapfrogging

14. The Communist Party of Peru, more commonly known as the _____ , is a Pseudo-Maoist guerrilla organization in Peru. When it first launched the internal conflict in Peru in 1980, its stated goal was to replace what it saw as bourgeois democracy with 'New Democracy.' The _____ believed that by imposing a dictatorship of the proletariat, inducing cultural revolution, and eventually sparking world revolution, they could arrive at pure communism. The _____ also believed that all existing socialist countries were revisionist, and that the _____ itself was the vanguard of the world communist movement.
   a. 100-year flood
   b. 1921 recession
   c. 130-30 fund
   d. Shining Path

15. In mathematics, a _____ is a constant multiplicative factor of a certain object. For example, in the expression $9x^2$, the _____ of x^2 is 9.

The object can be such things as a variable, a vector, a function, etc.

   a. 1921 recession
   b. 130-30 fund
   c. 100-year flood
   d. Coefficient

16. In mathematics, an _____ is a statement about the relative size or order of two objects, or about whether they are the same or not

   - The notation a < b means that a is less than b.
   - The notation a > b means that a is greater than b.
   - The notation a ≠ b means that a is not equal to b, but does not say that one is greater than the other or even that they can be compared in size.

In each statement above, a is not equal to b. These relations are known as strict inequalities. The notation a < b may also be read as 'a is strictly less than b'.

Chapter 13. Latin America: Argentina, Brazil, and Mexico

a. Inequality
b. ACCRA Cost of Living Index
c. AD-IA Model
d. ACEA agreement

17. _____ is the shortage of common things such as food, clothing, shelter and safe drinking water, all of which determine the quality of life. It may also include the lack of access to opportunities such as education and employment which aid the escape from _____ and/or allow one to enjoy the respect of fellow citizens. According to Mollie Orshansky who developed the _____ measurements used by the U.S. government, 'to be poor is to be deprived of those goods and services and pleasures which others around us take for granted.' Ongoing debates over causes, effects and best ways to measure _____, directly influence the design and implementation of _____-reduction programs and are therefore relevant to the fields of public administration and international development.
   a. Poverty map
   b. Poverty
   c. Liberal welfare reforms
   d. Growth Elasticity of Poverty

18. The _____ is a region that spans southwestern Asia and northeastern Africa. It has no clear boundaries, often used as a synonym to Near East, in opposition to Far East. The term '_____' was popularized around 1900 in the United Kingdom.
   a. 100-year flood
   b. 1921 recession
   c. 130-30 fund
   d. Middle East

19. _____ is

the belief or desire of a government or people that a country should maintain a strong military capability and be prepared to use it aggressively to defend or promote national interests.

It has also been defined as 'aggressiveness that involves the threat of using military force', and the

Glorification of the ideas of a professional military class' and 'Predominance of the armed forces in the administration or policy of the state

_____ has been a significant principle in the imperialist or expansionist ideologies of several nations throughout history. Some prominent examples are the Greek city state of Sparta, the Kingdom of Prussia, the British Empire, the Empire of Japan, the Russian Soviet Federative Socialist Republic , the Italian Colonial Empire during the reign of Benito Mussolini, Nazi Germany, and Iraq during the reign of Saddam Hussein.

   a. 1921 recession
   b. 130-30 fund
   c. 100-year flood
   d. Militarism

20. The _____ was a major armed struggle that started in 1910 with an uprising led by Francisco I. Madero against longtime autocrat Porfirio Díaz. The _____ was characterized by several socialist, liberal, anarchist, populist, and agrarianist movements.

The Revolution transformed itself from a revolt against the established order to a multi-sided civil war.

   a. 130-30 fund
   b. 1921 recession
   c. 100-year flood
   d. Mexican Revolution

Chapter 13. Latin America: Argentina, Brazil, and Mexico

21. _____ is a Regional Trade Agreement among Argentina, Brazil, Paraguay and Uruguay founded in 1991 by the Treaty of Asunci>ón, which was later amended and updated by the 1994 Treaty of Ouro Preto. Its purpose is to promote free trade and the fluid movement of goods, people, and currency.

_____ origins trace back to 1985 when Presidents Ra>úl Alfons>ín of Argentina and Jos>é Sarney of Brazil signed the Argentina-Brazil Integration and Economics Cooperation Program or PICE .

- a. 100-year flood
- b. Free trade area
- c. 130-30 fund
- d. MERCOSUR

22. The _____ is a trilateral trade bloc in North America created by the governments of the United States, Canada, and Mexico. The agreement creating the trade bloc came into force on January 1, 1994. It superseded the Canada-United States Free Trade Agreement between the U.S. and Canada.
- a. Demand-side technologies
- b. Federal Reserve Bank Notes
- c. North American Free Trade Agreement
- d. Case-Shiller Home Price Indices

23. _____ are usually numerical time-series, i.e., sets of data (covering periods of time) for part or all of a single economy or the international economy. When they are time-series the data sets are usually monthly but can be quarterly and annual. The data may be adjusted in various ways (for ease of further analysis), most commonly adjusted or unadjusted for seasonal fluctuations.
- a. ACEA agreement
- b. ACCRA Cost of Living Index
- c. AD-IA Model
- d. Economic data

24. _____ is the development of economic wealth of countries or regions for the well-being of their inhabitants. It is the process by which a nation improves the economic, political, and social well being of its people. From a policy perspective, _____ can be defined as efforts that seek to improve the economic well-being and quality of life for a community by creating and/or retaining jobs and supporting or growing incomes and the tax base.
- a. Economic methodology
- b. Inflation
- c. Experimental economics
- d. Economic development

25. _____: Kritik der politischen Ökonomie is an extensive treatise on political economy written in German by Karl Marx and edited in part by Friedrich Engels. The book is a critical analysis of capitalism. Its first volume was published in 1867.
- a. Capital accumulation
- b. Dialectics of Nature
- c. Das Kapital
- d. Productive force

26. The impact of the Mexican economic crisis on the Southern Cone and Brazil was labeled the _____ .

The crisis is also known in Spanish as el error de diciembre -- The December Mistake-- a term coined by the then ex-president Carlos Salinas de Gortari. While these critics agree that a devaluation was necessary, they argue that the way it was handled was politically incorrect .

- a. 130-30 fund
- b. 1921 recession
- c. 100-year flood
- d. Tequila effect

Chapter 13. Latin America: Argentina, Brazil, and Mexico

27. In finance, the _____s between two currencies specifies how much one currency is worth in terms of the other. It is the value of a foreign natione;s currency in terms of the home natione;s currency. For example an _____ of 102 Japanese yen to the United States dollar means that JPY 102 is worth the same as USD 1.

   a. Exchange rate
   c. ACCRA Cost of Living Index
   b. ACEA agreement
   d. Interbank market

28.

_____ was a German philosopher, political economist, historian, political theorist, sociologist, communist and revolutionary credited as the founder of communism.

Marx summarized his approach to history and politics in the opening line of the first chapter of The Communist Manifesto : e;The history of all hitherto existing society is the history of class struggles.e; Marx argued that capitalism, like previous socioeconomic systems, will produce internal tensions which will lead to its destruction. Just as capitalism replaced feudalism, socialism will in its turn replace capitalism and lead to a stateless, classless society which will emerge after a transitional period, the 'dictatorship of the proletariat'.

   a. Adam Smith
   c. Karl Heinrich Marx
   b. Marxism
   d. Neo-Gramscianism

29. _____ was an English writer on economics who has been called the last of the early mercantilists. He was among the first to recognize the exportation of service, or invisible items, as valuable trade, and made early statements strongly in support of capitalism.

Mun began his career by engaging in Mediterranean trade, and afterwards settled in London, amassing a large fortune.

   a. George Cabot Lodge II
   c. Thomas Mun
   b. Werner Sombart
   d. Henry Ford

30. _____ is an American economist and was the Chairman of the Federal Reserve of the United States from 1987 to 2006. He currently works as a private advisor and providing consulting for firms through his company, Greenspan Associates LLC.

First appointed Federal Reserve chairman by President Ronald Reagan in August 1987, he was reappointed at successive four-year intervals until retiring on January 31, 2006 after the second-longest tenure in the position.

   a. Alan Greenspan
   c. Adam Smith
   b. Adolph Fischer
   d. Adolf Hitler

31. There have been concerns over _____ over environmental and health and safety related issues as well as in respect of its businesses practices and priorities. In recent times Shelle;s management has acknowledged some of these problems and has promised to take steps to repair damage done both to the affected parties and to its own reputation, which has involved tightening internal controls between its different subsidiaries, an ostensible commitment to corporate social responsibility, an extensive global advertising campaign and other initiatives in the late 1990s and early 2000s.

Shell Austria and Shell Germany used forced labour at refineries in Vienna and Hamburg during the Nazi period, courtesy of the SS.

a. 100-year flood
b. 1921 recession
c. Royal Dutch Shell
d. 130-30 fund

32. _____ was a predominant American integrated oil producing, transporting, refining, and marketing company. Established in 1870 as an Ohio Corporation, it was the largest oil refiner in the world and operated as a major company trust and was one of the world's first and largest multinational corporations until it was broken up by the United States Supreme Court in 1911. John D. Rockefeller was a founder, chairman and major shareholder, and the company made him a billionaire and eventually the richest man in history.

a. 130-30 fund
b. Standard Oil
c. 100-year flood
d. 1921 recession

33. The _____ is the peace treaty, largely dictated by the United States to the interim government of a militarily occupied Mexico, that ended the Mexican-American War . The treaty provided for the Mexican Cession, in which Mexico ceded 1.36 million km^2 (525,000 square miles; 55% of its pre-war territory, not including Texas) to the United States in exchange for US$15 million (equivalent to $313 million in 2006 dollars) and the ensured safety of pre-existing property rights of Mexican citizens in the transferred territories. Despite assurances to the contrary, property rights of Mexican citizens were often not honored by the United States as per modifications to and interpretations of the treaty.

a. 100-year flood
b. Treaty of Guadalupe Hidalgo
c. 1921 recession
d. 130-30 fund

34. The _____ or gross domestic income (GDI), a basic measure of an economy's economic performance, is the market value of all final goods and services produced within the borders of a nation in a year. _____ can be defined in three ways, all of which are conceptually identical. First, it is equal to the total expenditures for all final goods and services produced within the country in a stipulated period of time (usually a 365-day year.)

a. Monopolistic competition
b. Market structure
c. Countercyclical
d. Gross domestic product

Chapter 14. Africa: Nigeria and South Africa

1. A variety of measures of national income and output are used in economics to estimate total economic activity in a country or region, including gross domestic product (GDP), _____ , and net national income (NNI.)

There are three main ways of calculating these numbers; the output approach, the income approach and the expenditure approach. In theory, the three must yield the same, because total expenditures on goods and services must equal the total income paid to the producers (GNI), and that must also equal the total value of the output of goods and services (_____.)

a. Household final consumption expenditure
b. Purchasing power parity
c. Gross world product
d. Gross national product

2. _____ has several particular meanings:

- in mathematics
    - _____ function
    - Euler _____
    - _____
    - _____ subgroup
    - method of _____s (partial differential equations)
- in physics and engineering
    - any _____ curve that shows the relationship between certain input- and output parameters, e.g.
    - an I-V or current-voltage _____ is the current in a circuit as a function of the applied voltage
    - Receiver-Operator _____
- in fiction
    - in Dungeons ' Dragons, _____ is another name for ability score

a. Characteristic
b. Technocracy
c. Russian financial crisis
d. Demand

3. _____ is the building and maintaining of colonies in one territory by people from another territory. Sovereignty over the colony is claimed by the metropole. Social structure, government and economics within the territory of the colony are changed by the colonists.
a. 1921 recession
b. Colonialism
c. 130-30 fund
d. 100-year flood

4. The _____ was one of the peace treaties at the end of World War I. It ended the state of war between Germany and the Allied Powers. It was signed on 28 June 1919, exactly five years after the assassination of Archduke Franz Ferdinand. The other Central Powers on the German side of World War I were dealt with in separate treaties.
a. 1921 recession
b. 100-year flood
c. 130-30 fund
d. Treaty of Versailles

5. _____, or a _____ is the concept of a resulting effect (cf. cause and effect, arising from another action. In general terms, it is used to indicate that all human actions, particularly crime and sin, have profound effects.
a. Solved
b. Consequence
c. Rule
d. Variability

Chapter 14. Africa: Nigeria and South Africa

6. A _____ is:

   - Rewrite _____, in generative grammar and computer science
   - Standardization, a formal and widely-accepted statement, fact, definition, or qualification
   - Operation, a determinate _____ for performing a mathematical operation and obtaining a certain result (Mathematics, Logic)
       - Unary operation
       - Binary operation
   - _____ of inference, a function from sets of formulae to formulae (Mathematics, Logic)
   - _____ of thumb, principle with broad application that is not intended to be strictly accurate or reliable for every situation. Also often simply referred to as a _____
   - Moral, an atomic element of a moral code for guiding choices in human behavior
   - Heuristic, a quantized '_____' which shows a tendency or probability for successful function
   - A regulation, as in sports
   - A Production _____, as in computer science
   - Procedural law, a _____ set governing the application of laws to cases
       - A law, which may informally be called a '_____'
       - A court ruling, a decision by a court
   - In the U.S. Government, a regulation mandated by Congress, but written or expanded upon by the Executive Branch.
   - Norm (sociology), an informal but widely accepted _____, concept, truth, definition, or qualification (social norms, legal norms, coding norms)
   - Norm (philosophy), a kind of sentence or a reason to act, feel or believe
   - 'Rulership' is the concept of governance by a government:
       - Military _____, governance by a military body
       - Monastic _____, a collection of precepts that guides the life of monks or nuns in a religious order where the superior holds the place of Christ
   - Slide _____

   - '_____,' a song by Ayumi Hamasaki
   - '_____,' a song by rapper Nas
   - '_____s,' an album by the band The Whitest Boy Alive
   - _____s: Pyaar Ka Superhit Formula, a 2003 Bollywood film
   - ruler, an instrument for measuring lengths
   - _____, a component of an astrolabe, circumferator or similar instrument
   - The _____s, a bestselling self-help book
   - _____ Project (Run Up-to-date Linux Everywhere), a project that aims to use up-to-date Linux software on old PCs
   - _____ engine, a software system that helps managing business _____s
   - Ja _____, a hip hop artist
       - R.U.L.E., a 2005 greatest hits album by rapper Ja _____
   - '_____s,' a KMFDM song

a. Rule   b. Technocracy
c. Demand   d. Procter ' Gamble

Chapter 14. Africa: Nigeria and South Africa

7. _____ is a voluntary transfer of resources from one country to another, given at least partly with the objective of benefiting the recipient country. It may have other functions as well: it may be given as a signal of diplomatic approval, or to strengthen a military ally, to reward a government for behaviour desired by the donor, to extend the donor's cultural influence, to provide infrastructure needed by the donor for resource extraction from the recipient country, or to gain other kinds of commercial access. Humanitarianism and altruism are, nevertheless, significant motivations for the giving of _____.

   a. ACCRA Cost of Living Index
   b. AID
   c. AD-IA Model
   d. ACEA agreement

8. The _____ is an international financial institution that provides financial and technical assistance to developing countries for development programs (e.g. bridges, roads, schools, etc.) with the stated goal of reducing poverty.

The _____ differs from the _____ Group, in that the _____ comprises only two institutions:

- International Bank for Reconstruction and Development (IBRD)
- International Development Association (IDA)

Whereas the latter incorporates these two in addition to three more:

- International Finance Corporation (IFC)
- Multilateral Investment Guarantee Agency (MIGA)
- International Centre for Settlement of Investment Disputes (ICSID)

John Maynard Keynes (right) represented the UK at the conference, and Harry Dexter White represented the US.

The _____ is one of two major financial institutions created as a result of the Bretton Woods Conference in 1944. The International Monetary Fund, a related but separate institution, is the second.

   a. Flow to Equity-Approach
   b. Financial costs of the 2003 Iraq War
   c. Bank-State-Branch
   d. World Bank

9. _____ is the shortage of common things such as food, clothing, shelter and safe drinking water, all of which determine the quality of life. It may also include the lack of access to opportunities such as education and employment which aid the escape from _____ and/or allow one to enjoy the respect of fellow citizens. According to Mollie Orshansky who developed the _____ measurements used by the U.S. government, 'to be poor is to be deprived of those goods and services and pleasures which others around us take for granted.' Ongoing debates over causes, effects and best ways to measure _____, directly influence the design and implementation of _____-reduction programs and are therefore relevant to the fields of public administration and international development.

   a. Liberal welfare reforms
   b. Growth Elasticity of Poverty
   c. Poverty
   d. Poverty map

10. _____ was a German Communist politician who led the German Democratic Republic from 1971 until 1989.

After German reunification, Honecker first fled to the Soviet Union but was extradited to Germany by the new Russian government. Back in Germany, he was imprisoned and tried for high treason and crimes committed during the Cold War.

a. Erich Honecker
b. Adam Smith
c. Adolph Fischer
d. Adolf Hitler

11. The _____ is an index used to rank countries by level of 'human development', which usually also implies whether a country is a developed, developing, or underdeveloped country.

The _____ combines normalized measures of life expectancy, literacy, educational attainment, and GDP per capita for countries worldwide. It is claimed as a standard means of measuring human development--a concept that, according to the United Nations Development Program (UNDP), refers to the process of widening the options of persons, giving them greater opportunities for education, health care, income, employment, etc.

a. 1921 recession
b. 130-30 fund
c. 100-year flood
d. Human Development Index

12. _____ or development cooperation (also development assistance, technical assistance, international aid, overseas aid or foreign aid) is aid given by governments and other agencies to support the economic, social and political development of developing countries. It is distinguished from humanitarian aid as being aimed at alleviating poverty in the long term, rather than alleviating suffering in the short term. The term development cooperation, which is used, for example, by the World Health Organisation (WHO) is used to express the idea that a partnership should exist between donor and recipient, rather than the traditional situation in which the relationship was dominated by the wealth and specialised knowldge of one side.

a. Legatum Prosperity Index
b. Capacity Development
c. Development AID
d. Multilateral development bank

13. _____ is the branch of life sciences that studies short- and long-term changes in the size and age composition of populations, and the biological and environmental processes influencing those changes. _____ deals with the way populations are affected by birth and death rates, and by immigration and emigration, and studies topics such as aging populations or population decline.

_____ has traditionally been the dominant branch of mathematical biology, which has a history of more than 210 years, although more recently the scope of mathematical biology has greatly expanded.

a. 100-year flood
b. Population growth
c. 130-30 fund
d. Population dynamics

14. Marxist philosophy or _____ are terms which cover work in philosophy which is strongly influenced by Karl Marx's materialist approach to theory or which is written by Marxists. It may be broadly divided into Western Marxism, which drew out of various sources, and the official philosophy in the Soviet Union, which enforced a rigid reading of Marx called 'diamat' (for 'dialectical materialism'), in particular during the 1930s. The phrase 'Marxist philosophy' itself does not indicate a strictly defined sub-field of philosophy, because the diverse influence of _____ has extended into fields as diverse as aesthetics, ethics, ontology, epistemology, and philosophy of science, as well as its obvious influence on political philosophy and the philosophy of history.
   a. 130-30 fund
   b. 1921 recession
   c. 100-year flood
   d. Marxist theory

15. In mathematics, an _____ is a statement about the relative size or order of two objects, or about whether they are the same or not

   - The notation a < b means that a is less than b.
   - The notation a > b means that a is greater than b.
   - The notation a ≠ b means that a is not equal to b, but does not say that one is greater than the other or even that they can be compared in size.

In each statement above, a is not equal to b. These relations are known as strict inequalities. The notation a < b may also be read as 'a is strictly less than b'.

   a. ACCRA Cost of Living Index
   b. ACEA agreement
   c. Inequality
   d. AD-IA Model

16. A _____ is the procedure of systematically acquiring and recording information about the members of a given population. It is a regularly occurring and official count of a particular population. The term is used mostly in connection with national 'population and door to door _____es' (to be taken every 10 years according to United Nations recommendations), agriculture, and business _____es.
   a. 100-year flood
   b. 130-30 fund
   c. Census
   d. 1921 recession

17. In economics, _____ is how a natione;s total economy is distributed among its population. ._____ has always been a central concern of economic theory and economic policy. Classical economists such as Adam Smith, Thomas Malthus and David Ricardo were mainly concerned with factor _____, that is, the distribution of income between the main factors of production, land, labour and capital.
   a. Equipment trust certificate
   b. Authorised capital
   c. Eco commerce
   d. Income distribution

18. _____ is a broad label that refers to any individuals or households that use goods and services generated within the economy. The concept of a _____ is used in different contexts, so that the usage and significance of the term may vary.

Typically when business people and economists talk of _____s they are talking about person as _____, an aggregated commodity item with little individuality other than that expressed in the buy/not-buy decision.

a. 1921 recession
b. Consumer
c. 130-30 fund
d. 100-year flood

19. _____ was a Swedish economist and politician. He was a professor of economics at the Stockholm School of Economics from 1929 to 1965. He was also leader of the People's Party, a social-liberal party which at the time was the largest party in opposition to the governing Social Democratic Party, from 1944 to 1967.
   a. Nicholas II
   b. Martin Luther
   c. Maximilian Carl Emil Weber
   d. Bertil Gotthard Ohlin

20. _____s is the social science that studies the production, distribution, and consumption of goods and services. The term _____s comes from the Ancient Greek oá¼°κονομῖα from oá¼¶κος (oikos, 'house') + vÏŒμος (nomos, 'custom' or 'law'), hence 'rules of the house(hold)'. Current _____ models developed out of the broader field of political economy in the late 19th century, owing to a desire to use an empirical approach more akin to the physical sciences.
   a. Energy economics
   b. Opportunity cost
   c. Economic
   d. Inflation

21. _____ are usually numerical time-series, i.e., sets of data (covering periods of time) for part or all of a single economy or the international economy. When they are time-series the data sets are usually monthly but can be quarterly and annual. The data may be adjusted in various ways (for ease of further analysis), most commonly adjusted or unadjusted for seasonal fluctuations.
   a. ACEA agreement
   b. Economic data
   c. AD-IA Model
   d. ACCRA Cost of Living Index

Chapter 15. World Economic Integration

1. The Caribbean Community (_____), is an organisation of 15 Caribbean nations and dependencies. _____'s main purposes are to promote economic integration and cooperation among its members, to ensure that the benefits of integration are equitably shared, and to coordinate foreign policy. Its major activities involve coordinating economic policies and development planning; devising and instituting special projects for the less-developed countries within its jurisdiction; operating as a regional single market for many of its members (_____ Single Market); and handling regional trade disputes.
    a. 100-year flood
    b. 1921 recession
    c. 130-30 fund
    d. CARICOM

2. The _____, is an organisation of 15 Caribbean nations and dependencies. CARICOM's main purposes are to promote economic integration and cooperation among its members, to ensure that the benefits of integration are equitably shared, and to coordinate foreign policy. Its major activities involve coordinating economic policies and development planning; devising and instituting special projects for the less-developed countries within its jurisdiction; operating as a regional single market for many of its members (Caricom Single Market); and handling regional trade disputes.
    a. 1921 recession
    b. Caribbean Community
    c. 100-year flood
    d. 130-30 fund

3. _____ is a type of trade policy that allows traders to act and transact without interference from government. Thus, the policy permits trading partners mutual gains from trade, with goods and services produced according to the theory of comparative advantage.

   Under a _____ policy, prices are a reflection of true supply and demand, and are the sole determinant of resource allocation.

    a. 100-year flood
    b. Free Trade
    c. 1921 recession
    d. 130-30 fund

4. The _____ is a trilateral trade bloc in North America created by the governments of the United States, Canada, and Mexico. The agreement creating the trade bloc came into force on January 1, 1994. It superseded the Canada-United States Free Trade Agreement between the U.S. and Canada.
    a. Demand-side technologies
    b. Federal Reserve Bank Notes
    c. Case-Shiller Home Price Indices
    d. North American Free Trade Agreement

5. _____ is a socioeconomic structure and political ideology that promotes the establishment of an egalitarian, classless, stateless society based on common ownership and control of the means of production and property in general. In political science, the term '_____' is sometimes used to refer to communist states, a form of government in which the state operates under a one-party system and declares allegiance to Marxism-Leninism or a derivative thereof, even if the party does not actually claim that it has already reached _____.

   Forerunners of communist ideas existed in antiquity and particularly in the 18th and early 19th century France, with thinkers such as Jean-Jacques Rousseau and the more radical Gracchus Babeuf.

    a. Democratic centralism
    b. Social fascism
    c. New Communist Movement
    d. Communism

Chapter 15. World Economic Integration

6. _____s is the social science that studies the production, distribution, and consumption of goods and services. The term _____s comes from the Ancient Greek oá¼°κονομῖα from oá¼¶κος (oikos, 'house') + vÏŒμος (nomos, 'custom' or 'law'), hence 'rules of the house(hold)'. Current _____ models developed out of the broader field of political economy in the late 19th century, owing to a desire to use an empirical approach more akin to the physical sciences.
   a. Energy economics
   b. Opportunity cost
   c. Inflation
   d. Economic

7. _____ is a term used to describe how different aspects between economies are integrated. The basics of this theory were written by the Hungarian Economist Béla Balassa in the 1960s. As _____ increases, the barriers of trade between markets diminishes.
   a. Import license
   b. Import
   c. Inward investment
   d. Economic integration

8. A _____ is a customs union with common policies on product regulation, and freedom of movement of the factors of production (capital and labour) and of enterprise. The goal is that the movement of capital, labour, goods, and services between the members is as easy as within them. This is the fourth stage of economic integration.
   a. Competitiveness
   b. Mutual recognition agreement
   c. Grey market
   d. Common Market

9. The _____, is a preferential trading area with nineteen member states stretching from Libya to Zimbabwe. COMESA formed in December 1994, replacing a Preferential Trade Area which had existed since 1981. Nine of the member states formed a free trade area in 2000, with Rwanda and Burundi joining the FTA in 2004 and the Comoros and Libya in 2006.
   a. Common Market for Eastern and Southern Africa
   b. 130-30 fund
   c. 100-year flood
   d. 1921 recession

10. _____ describes a deliberate attempt to interfere with the free and fair operation of the market and create artificial, false or misleading appearances with respect to the price of a security, commodity or currency. _____ is prohibited under Section 9(a)(2) of the Securities Exchange Act of 1934, and in Australia under Section s 1041A of the Corporations Act 2001. The Act defines _____ as transactions which create an artificial price or maintain an artificial price for a tradable security.
    a. Net domestic product
    b. Legal monopoly
    c. Managerial economics
    d. Market manipulation

11. A _____ is a free trade area with a common external tariff. The participant countries set up common external trade policy, but in some cases they use different import quotas. Common competition policy is also helpful to avoid competition deficiency.
    a. Common market
    b. Customs union
    c. Bilateral Investment Treaty
    d. Grey market

12. A _____ is a type of state which is composed of or created out of smaller states. Unlike a personal union, the individual states share a common government and the union is recognized internationally as a single political entity. A _____ may also be called a legislative union or state union.
    a. Linestanding
    b. Dirty subsidy
    c. Soft power
    d. Political union

13. _____ is the shortage of common things such as food, clothing, shelter and safe drinking water, all of which determine the quality of life. It may also include the lack of access to opportunities such as education and employment which aid the escape from _____ and/or allow one to enjoy the respect of fellow citizens. According to Mollie Orshansky who developed the _____ measurements used by the U.S. government, 'to be poor is to be deprived of those goods and services and pleasures which others around us take for granted.' Ongoing debates over causes, effects and best ways to measure _____, directly influence the design and implementation of _____-reduction programs and are therefore relevant to the fields of public administration and international development.

a. Poverty
b. Liberal welfare reforms
c. Growth Elasticity of Poverty
d. Poverty map

14. A _____ or labor union is an organization of workers who have banded together to achieve common goals in key areas and working conditions. The _____, through its leadership, bargains with the employer on behalf of union members (rank and file members) and negotiates labor contracts (Collective bargaining) with employers. This may include the negotiation of wages, work rules, complaint procedures, rules governing hiring, firing and promotion of workers, benefits, workplace safety and policies.

a. Case-Shiller Home Price Indices
b. Consumer goods
c. Guaranteed investment contracts
d. Trade union

15. The _____, published in 1998 (with an epilogue added to the 1999 paperback edition), is a book by David Landes, currently Emeritus Professor of Economics and former Coolidge Professor of History at Harvard University. In it, Landes explains the 'European Miracle', or why European societies experienced a period of explosive growth when the rest of the world did not.

In doing so, he revives, at least in part, several theories he believes have been unfairly discarded by academics over the last 40 years.

a. Wealth and poverty of nations
b. The General Theory of Employment, Interest and Money
c. Human Action
d. Banks and Politics in America

16. The _____ was a six-nation international organisation serving to unify Western Europe during the Cold War and creating the foundation for European democracy and the modern-day developments of the European Union. The ECSC was the first organisation to be based on the principles of supranationalism.

The ECSC was first proposed by French foreign minister Robert Schuman on 9 May 1950 as a way to prevent further war between France and Germany.

a. European Coal and Steel Community
b. ACCRA Cost of Living Index
c. AD-IA Model
d. ACEA agreement

17. _____ is sometimes referred to as _____, actually it means Economic Monetary Union.

First ideas of an economic and monetary union in Europe were raised well before establishing the European Communities. For example, already in the League of Nations, Gustav Stresemann asked in 1929 for a European currency (Link) against the background of an increased economic division due to a number of new nation states in Europe after WWI.

Chapter 15. World Economic Integration

a. Exchange rate mechanism
b. Euro Interbank Offered Rate
c. European Monetary Union
d. European Monetary System

18. The _____ is an economic and political union of 27 member states, located primarily in Europe. It was established by the Treaty of Maastricht on 1 November 1993, upon the foundations of the pre-existing European Economic Community. With a population of almost 500 million, the _____ generates an estimated 30% share (US$18.4 trillion in 2008) of the nominal gross world product.
   a. European Court of Justice
   b. ACCRA Cost of Living Index
   c. European Union
   d. ACEA agreement

19. An economic and _____ is a single market with a common currency. It is to be distinguished from a mere currency union, which does not involve a single market. This is the fifth stage of economic integration.
   a. Customs union
   b. Free trade zone
   c. Commercial invoice
   d. Monetary Union

20. The _____ are two of the treaties of the European Union signed on March 25, 1957. Both treaties were signed by The Six: Belgium, France, Italy, Luxembourg, the Netherlands and West Germany.

The first established the European Economic Community and the second established the European Atomic Energy Community (EAEC or Euratom.)

   a. 100-year flood
   b. Maastricht Treaty
   c. Treaty of Amsterdam
   d. Treaties of Rome

21. _____ is money accepted for exchange of goods in an economy. The prevalence of one money over another arises, usually, when a government designates through decrees that the government shall accept only particular notes and coins in payment for taxes. Typically, money of _____ consists of stamped coins and minted paper bills.
   a. Security thread
   b. Local currency
   c. Currency
   d. Totnes pound

22. The _____ was a basket of the currencies of the European Community member states, used as the unit of account of the European Community before being replaced by the euro on January 1, 1999, at parity. The _____ itself replaced the European Unit of Account, also at parity, on March 13, 1979. The European Exchange Rate Mechanism attempted to minimize fluctuations between member state currencies and the _____.
   a. ACCRA Cost of Living Index
   b. ACEA agreement
   c. European Currency Unit
   d. AD-IA Model

23. _____ was an arrangement established in 1979 under the Jenkins European Commission where most nations of the European Economic Community (EEC) linked their currencies to prevent large fluctuations relative to one another.

After the collapse of the Bretton Woods system in 1971, most of the EEC countries agreed in 1972 to maintain stable exchange rates by preventing exchange fluctuations of more than 2.25% (the European 'currency snake'.) In March 1979, this system was replaced by the _____, and the European Currency Unit (ECU) was defined.

a. European Monetary Union
b. Exchange rate mechanism
c. Euro Interbank Offered Rate
d. European Monetary System

24. A _____ secures the proper functioning of money by regulating economic agents, transaction types, and money supply.

_____s are traditionally formed by the policy decisions of individual governments and administrated as a domestic economic issue.

The current trend, however, is to use international trade and investment to alter the policy and legislation of individual governments.

a. Financial rand
b. Consumer basket
c. Netting
d. Monetary System

25. In finance, the _____s between two currencies specifies how much one currency is worth in terms of the other. It is the value of a foreign natione;s currency in terms of the home natione;s currency. For example an _____ of 102 Japanese yen to the United States dollar means that JPY 102 is worth the same as USD 1.

a. ACEA agreement
b. Exchange rate
c. Interbank market
d. ACCRA Cost of Living Index

26. The European _____, was a system introduced by the European Community in March 1979, as part of the European Monetary System (EMS), to reduce exchange rate variability and achieve monetary stability in Europe, in preparation for Economic and Monetary Union and the introduction of a single currency, the euro, which took place on 1 January 1999. Subsequent exchange rate agreements made with countries wishing to join the Eurozone are known as _____ II.

The _____ is based on the concept of fixed currency exchange rate margins, but with exchange rates variable within those margins.

a. Euro Interbank Offered Rate
b. European Monetary System
c. European Monetary Union
d. Exchange rate mechanism

27. A _____, reserve bank, or monetary authority is the entity responsible for the monetary policy of a country or of a group of member states. It is a bank that can lend money to other banks in times of need. Its primary responsibility is to maintain the stability of the national currency and money supply, but more active duties include controlling subsidized-loan interest rates, and acting as a lender of last resort to the banking sector during times of financial crisis (private banks often being integral to the national financial system.)

a. 1921 recession
b. 100-year flood
c. Central Bank
d. 130-30 fund

28. The _____ is one of the world's most important central banks, responsible for monetary policy covering the 16 member States of the Eurozone. It was established by the European Union (EU) in 1998 with its headquarters in Frankfurt, Germany.

The predecessor to the _____ was the European Monetary Institute .

Chapter 15. World Economic Integration

a. AD-IA Model
b. ACCRA Cost of Living Index
c. European Central Bank
d. ACEA agreement

29. The _____ was signed on 7 February 1992 in Maastricht, the Netherlands after final negotiations on 9 December 1991 between the members of the European Community and entered into force on 1 November 1993 during the Delors Commission. It created the European Union and led to the creation of the euro. The _____ has been amended to a degree by later treaties.
    a. Maastricht Treaty
    b. Treaty of Amsterdam
    c. 100-year flood
    d. Treaties of Rome

30. The _____ amending the Treaty of the European Union, the Treaties establishing the European Communities and certain related acts, commonly known as the Amsterdam Treaty, was signed on 2 October 1997, and entered into force on 1 May 1999; it made substantial changes to the Treaty on European Union, which had been signed at Maastricht in 1992.

The Amsterdam Treaty meant a greater emphasis on citizenship and the rights of individuals, an attempt to achieve more democracy in the shape of increased powers for the European Parliament, a new title on employment, a Community area of freedom, security and justice, the beginnings of a common foreign and security policy (CFSP) and the reform of the institutions in the run-up to enlargement.

The treaty was the result of very long negotiations which began in Messina, Sicily on 2 June 1995, nearly forty years after the signing of the Treaties of Rome, and reached completion in Amsterdam on 18 June 1997.

  a. 100-year flood
  b. Treaties of Rome
  c. Treaty of Amsterdam
  d. Maastricht Treaty

31. The _____ is the official currency of 16 of the 27 member states of the European Union (EU.) The states, known collectively as the Eurozone, are Austria, Belgium, Cyprus, Finland, France, Germany, Greece, Ireland, Italy, Luxembourg, Malta, the Netherlands, Portugal, Slovakia, Slovenia, and Spain. The currency is also used in a further five European countries, with and without formal agreements and is consequently used daily by some 327 million Europeans.
    a. Import and Export Price Indices
    b. Equity capital market
    c. Euro
    d. IRS Code 3401

32. The _____ is the principal decision-making institution of the European Union (EU.) It is often informally called the Council of Ministers or just the Council, the name used in the treaties; it is also called Consilium as a Latin-language compromise. Within the competencies of the Community pillar, it is the more powerful of the two legislative chambers, the other being the European Parliament.
    a. 100-year flood
    b. Council of the European Union
    c. Treaty of Amsterdam
    d. Maastricht Treaty

33. The Court of Justice of the European Communities, usually called the _____, is the highest court in the European Union in matters of European Community law. It has the ultimate say on matters of EU law in order to ensure its equal application across all EU member states.

The court was established in 1952 and is -- unlike most other Union institutions -- based in Luxembourg.

Chapter 15. World Economic Integration

a. ACEA agreement
b. ACCRA Cost of Living Index
c. European Union
d. European Court of Justice

34. In finance, the term _____ describes various legal measures taken to ensure that debtors, whether individuals, businesses honor their debts and make an honest effort to repay the money that they owe. Generally regarded as a subdivision of tax law, _____ is most often enforced through a combination of audits and legal restrictions. For example, a provision of the Federal Debt Collection Procedure Act states that a person or organization indebted to the United States, against whom a judgment lien has been filed, is ineligible to receive a government grant.

a. Hard money loan
b. Microcredit
c. Debt compliance
d. Carryback loan

35. A _____ is a broad coalition government consisting of all parties (or all major parties) in the legislature, usually formed during a time of war or other national emergency.

During World War I the Conservative government of Sir Robert Borden invited the Liberal opposition to join the government as a means of dealing with the Conscription crisis of 1917. The Liberals, led by Sir Wilfrid Laurier refused; however, Borden was able to convince many individual Liberals to join what was called a Union Government, which defeated the Laurier Liberals in the fall 1917 election.

a. 100-year flood
b. 1921 recession
c. 130-30 fund
d. National government

36. _____ for goods in the WTO means the conditions, tariff and non-tariff measures, agreed by members for the entry of specific goods into their markets. Tariff commitments for goods are set out in each member's schedules of concessions on goods. The schedules represent commitments not to apply tariffs above the listed rates -- these rates are e;bounde;.

a. Merchant bank
b. Jamaican Free Zones
c. Heckscher-Ohlin model
d. Market access

37. The Great Proletarian _____ in the People's Republic of China was a period of widespread social and political upheaval; the nation-wide chaos and economic disarray engulfed much of Chinese society between 1966 and 1976.

It was launched by Mao Zedong, the chairman of the Communist Party of China, on May 16, 1966, who alleged that liberal bourgeoisie elements were dominating the party and insisted that they needed to be removed through post-revolutionary class struggle by mobilizing the thoughts and actions of China's youth, who formed Red Guards groups around the country. Although Mao himself officially declared the _____ to have ended in 1969, today it is widely believed that the power struggles and political instability between 1969 and the arrest of the Gang of Four as well as the death of Mao in 1976 were also part of the Revolution.

a. 1921 recession
b. 100-year flood
c. Cultural Revolution
d. 130-30 fund

38. _____, in law and economics, is a form of risk management primarily used to hedge against the risk of a contingent loss. _____ is defined as the equitable transfer of the risk of a loss, from one entity to another, in exchange for a premium, and can be thought of as a guaranteed small loss to prevent a large, possibly devastating loss. An insurer is a company selling the _____; an insured or policyholder is the person or entity buying the _____.

Chapter 15. World Economic Integration

a. ACCRA Cost of Living Index
b. AD-IA Model
c. ACEA agreement
d. Insurance

39. _____ are legal property rights over creations of the mind, both artistic and commercial, and the corresponding fields of law. Under _____ law, owners are granted certain exclusive rights to a variety of intangible assets, such as musical, literary, and artistic works; ideas, discoveries and inventions; and words, phrases, symbols, and designs. Common types of _____ include copyrights, trademarks, patents, industrial design rights and trade secrets.
 a. Independent contractor
 b. Ease of Doing Business Index
 c. Expedited Funds Availability Act
 d. Intellectual property

40. A _____ is the exclusive authority to determine how a resource is used, whether that resource is owned by government or by individuals. All economic goods have a _____s attribute. This attribute has three broad components

 1. The right to use the good
 2. The right to earn income from the good
 3. The right to transfer the good to others

The concept of _____s as used by economists and legal scholars are related but distinct. The distinction is largely seen in the economists' focus on the ability of an individual or collective to control the use of the good.

 a. Post-sale restraint
 b. Holder in due course
 c. High-reeve
 d. Property right

41. In microeconomics, _____ is quite simply the conversion of inputs into outputs. It is an economic process that uses resources to create a good or service that is suitable for exchange. This can include manufacturing, storing, shipping, and packaging.
 a. Solved
 b. MET
 c. Red Guards
 d. Production

42. _____ in economics refers to metrics and measures of output from production processes, per unit of input. Labor _____, for example, is typically measured as a ratio of output per labor-hour, an input. _____ may be conceived of as a metrics of the technical or engineering efficiency of production.
 a. Productivity
 b. Piece work
 c. Fordism
 d. Production-possibility frontier

43. _____ is a Regional Trade Agreement among Argentina, Brazil, Paraguay and Uruguay founded in 1991 by the Treaty of Asunci>ón, which was later amended and updated by the 1994 Treaty of Ouro Preto. Its purpose is to promote free trade and the fluid movement of goods, people, and currency.

_____ origins trace back to 1985 when Presidents Ra>úl Alfons>ín of Argentina and Jos>é Sarney of Brazil signed the Argentina-Brazil Integration and Economics Cooperation Program or PICE .

 a. 100-year flood
 b. MERCOSUR
 c. Free trade area
 d. 130-30 fund

Chapter 15. World Economic Integration

44. _____ is a forum for 21 Pacific Rim countries (styled 'member economies') to cooperate on regional trade and investment liberalisation and facilitation. APEC's objective is to enhance economic growth and prosperity in the region and to strengthen the Asia-Pacific community. Members account for approximately 40% of the world's population, approximately 54% of world GDP and about 44% of world trade.
   a. ACEA agreement
   b. Asia-Pacific Economic Cooperation
   c. ACCRA Cost of Living Index
   d. AD-IA Model

45. Asia-Pacific Economic Cooperation is a forum for 21 Pacific Rim countries (styled 'member economies') to cooperate on regional trade and investment liberalisation and facilitation. _____'s objective is to enhance economic growth and prosperity in the region and to strengthen the Asia-Pacific community. Members account for approximately 40% of the world's population, approximately 54% of world GDP and about 44% of world trade.
   a. AD-IA Model
   b. ACCRA Cost of Living Index
   c. ACEA agreement
   d. Asian Pacific Economic Cooperation

46. A _____ is crossing the border without being taxed for it.

A _____ or export processing zone (EPZ) is one or more special areas of a country where some normal trade barriers such as tariffs and quotas are eliminated and bureaucratic requirements are lowered in hopes of attracting new business and foreign investments. It is a a region where a group of countries has agreed to reduce or eliminate trade barriers.

   a. Competitiveness
   b. Free trade zone
   c. Heckscher-Ohlin model
   d. Most favoured nation

47. The _____ is a trade agreement between Non-EU countries in Central and South-Eastern Europe.

As of 1 May 2007, the parties of the _____ agreement are: Albania, Bosnia and Herzegovina, Croatia, Macedonia, Moldova, Montenegro, Serbia and UNMIK.

Former parties are Bulgaria, the Czech Republic, Hungary, Poland, Romania, Slovakia and Slovenia.

   a. Congress of Industrial Organizations
   b. CEFTA
   c. Multinational corporation
   d. National Bureau of Economic Research

48. _____ is a free trade agreement between the governments of New Zealand and Australia. It is also known as the Australia New Zealand _____ Trade Agreement (ANZCloser Economic RelationsTA.) It came into force on 1 January 1983, although the actual treaty was not signed until 28 March 1983 by Deputy Prime Minister of Australia and Minister for Trade, Lionel Bowen and New Zealand High Commissioner to Australia, Laurie Francis in Canberra, Australia.
   a. 130-30 fund
   b. 100-year flood
   c. MERCOSUR
   d. Closer Economic Relations

49. The _____ , 1949-1991, was an economic organization of communist states and a kind of Eastern Bloc equivalent to--but more geographically inclusive than--the European Economic Community. The military equivalent to the Comecon was the Warsaw Pact, though Comecon's membership was significantly wider. The Comecon was the Eastern Bloc's reply to the formation of the OEEC .

a. 1921 recession
b. Council for Mutual Economic Assistance
c. 130-30 fund
d. 100-year flood

50. _____ is a designated group of countries that have agreed to eliminate tariffs, quotas and preferences on most (if not all) goods and services traded between them. It can be considered the second stage of economic integration. Countries choose this kind of economic integration form if their economical structures are complementary.
a. Free Trade Area
b. 130-30 fund
c. MERCOSUR
d. 100-year flood

51. The _____ is the central bank of the Federal Republic of Germany and as such part of the European System of Central Banks . Due to its strength and former size, the Bundesbank is the most influential member of the ESCB. Both the _____ and the European Central Bank (ECB) are located in Frankfurt am Main.
a. Deutsche Bundesbank
b. 130-30 fund
c. 1921 recession
d. 100-year flood

Chapter 16. The Twenty-First Century

1. _____ was a global military conflict which involved a majority of the world's nations, including all of the great powers, organized into two opposing military alliances: the Allies and the Axis. The war involved the mobilization of over 100 million military personnel, making it the most widespread war in history. In a state of 'total war', the major participants placed their entire economic, industrial, and scientific capabilities at the service of the war effort, erasing the distinction between civilian and military resources.
   - a. 130-30 fund
   - b. 1921 recession
   - c. 100-year flood
   - d. World War II

2. The term _____ commonly refers to the total number of living humans on Earth at a given time. As of May 2009, the Earth's population is 6,634,236,512. The _____ has been growing continuously since the end of the Black Death around 1400..
   - a. World Population
   - b. Adolph Fischer
   - c. Adam Smith
   - d. Adolf Hitler

3. The _____ was a physical barrier completely encircling West Berlin, separating it from the German Democratic Republic, including East Berlin. The longer inner German border demarcated the border between East and West Germany. Both borders came to symbolize the Iron Curtain between Western Europe and the Eastern Bloc.
   - a. Cold War
   - b. Sino-Soviet split
   - c. Reagan Doctrine
   - d. Berlin Wall

4. _____: Kritik der politischen Ökonomie is an extensive treatise on political economy written in German by Karl Marx and edited in part by Friedrich Engels. The book is a critical analysis of capitalism. Its first volume was published in 1867.
   - a. Dialectics of Nature
   - b. Das Kapital
   - c. Capital accumulation
   - d. Productive force

5. Crude _____ is the nativity or childbirths per 1,000 people per year.

It can be represented by number of childbirths in that year, and p is the current population. This figure is combined with the crude death rate to produce the rate of natural population growth (natural in that it does not take into account net migration.)

   - a. Depensation
   - b. Birth rate
   - c. Neo-Malthusianism
   - d. Malthusian equilibrium

6. In economics, the people in the _____ are the suppliers of labor. The _____ is all the nonmilitary people who are employed or unemployed. In 2005, the worldwide _____ was over 3 billion people.
   - a. Departmentalization
   - b. Distributed workforce
   - c. Grenelle agreements
   - d. Labor force

7. _____ is a voluntary transfer of resources from one country to another, given at least partly with the objective of benefiting the recipient country. It may have other functions as well: it may be given as a signal of diplomatic approval, or to strengthen a military ally, to reward a government for behaviour desired by the donor, to extend the donor's cultural influence, to provide infrastructure needed by the donor for resource extraction from the recipient country, or to gain other kinds of commercial access. Humanitarianism and altruism are, nevertheless, significant motivations for the giving of _____.
   - a. AID
   - b. AD-IA Model
   - c. ACCRA Cost of Living Index
   - d. ACEA agreement

8. The _____ established the Federal Deposit Insurance Corporation (FDIC) in the United States and included banking reforms, some of which were designed to control speculation. Some provisions such as Regulation Q, which allowed the Federal Reserve to regulate interest rates in savings accounts, were repealed by the Depository Institutions Deregulation and Monetary Control Act of 1980. Provisions that prohibit a bank holding company from owning other financial companies were repealed on November 12, 1999, by the Gramm-Leach-Bliley Act.
   a. 1921 recession
   b. Glass-Steagall Act of 1933
   c. 130-30 fund
   d. 100-year flood

9. _____ is the logging and/or burning of trees in a forested area. There are several reasons for doing so: trees or derived charcoal can be sold as a commodity and used by humans, while cleared land is used as pasture, plantations of commodities and human settlement. The removal of trees without sufficient reforestation has resulted in damage to habitat, biodiversity loss and aridity.
   a. Green New Deal
   b. Joint Implementation
   c. Deforestation
   d. Greenhouse gases

10. _____ is the increase in the average temperature of the Earth's near-surface air and oceans since the mid-twentieth century and its projected continuation. Global surface temperature increased 0.74 ± 0.18 °C (1.33 ± 0.32 °F) during the last century. The Intergovernmental Panel on Climate Change (IPCC) concludes that anthropogenic greenhouse gases are responsible for most of the observed temperature increase since the middle of the twentieth century, and that natural phenomena such as solar variation and volcanoes probably had a small warming effect from pre-industrial times to 1950 and a small cooling effect afterward.
   a. Controlled Foreign Corporations
   b. Global warming
   c. Consumer goods
   d. Dividend unit

11. Rainforests are forests characterized by high rainfall, with definitions setting minimum normal annual rainfall between 1750-2000 mm (68-78 inches.) The monsoon trough, alternately known as the intertropical convergence zone, plays a significant role in creating Earth's tropical _____.

From 40 to 75% of all species on Earth are indigenous to the rainforests.

   a. 1921 recession
   b. 100-year flood
   c. 130-30 fund
   d. Rain forests

12. _____, born in Newtown, Montgomeryshire, Wales was a social reformer and one of the founders of socialism and the cooperative movement.

Owen's philosophy was based on three intellectual pillars:

- First, no one was responsible for his will and his own actions, because his whole character is formed independently of himself; people are products of their environment, hence his support for education and labour reform, rendering him a pioneer in human capital investment.
- Second, all religions are based on the same absurd imagination, that make man a weak, imbecile animal; a furious bigot and fanatic; or a miserable hypocrite; (in dotage, he embraced Spiritualism.)
- Third, support for the putting-out system instead of the factory system.

Owen was born in Newtown, then a small market town in Montgomeryshire, Mid Wales, the sixth child of seven. His father had a small business as a saddler and ironmonger. Owen's mother came from one of the prosperous farming families; here, young Owen received almost all his school education, which terminated at the age of ten.

a. Adam Smith
b. Robert Owen
c. Adolf Hitler
d. Adolph Fischer

13. _____s is the social science that studies the production, distribution, and consumption of goods and services. The term _____s comes from the Ancient Greek oá¼°κονομῑα from oá¼¶κος (oikos, 'house') + vĺŒμος (nomos, 'custom' or 'law'), hence 'rules of the house(hold)'. Current _____ models developed out of the broader field of political economy in the late 19th century, owing to a desire to use an empirical approach more akin to the physical sciences.

a. Economic
b. Opportunity cost
c. Energy economics
d. Inflation

14. _____ is the development of economic wealth of countries or regions for the well-being of their inhabitants. It is the process by which a nation improves the economic, political, and social well being of its people. From a policy perspective, _____ can be defined as efforts that seek to improve the economic well-being and quality of life for a community by creating and/or retaining jobs and supporting or growing incomes and the tax base.

a. Economic methodology
b. Inflation
c. Experimental economics
d. Economic development

15. In mathematics, an _____ is a statement about the relative size or order of two objects, or about whether they are the same or not

- The notation a < b means that a is less than b.
- The notation a > b means that a is greater than b.
- The notation a ≠ b means that a is not equal to b, but does not say that one is greater than the other or even that they can be compared in size.

In each statement above, a is not equal to b. These relations are known as strict inequalities. The notation a < b may also be read as 'a is strictly less than b'.

a. AD-IA Model
b. ACCRA Cost of Living Index
c. ACEA agreement
d. Inequality

16. _____ refers to a business or organization attempting to acquire goods or services to accomplish the goals of the enterprise. Though there are several organizations that attempt to set standards in the _____ process, processes can vary greatly between organizations. Typically the word '_____' is not used interchangeably with the word 'procurement', since procurement typically includes Expediting, Supplier Quality, and Traffic and Logistics (T'L) in addition to _____.

a. Purchasing
b. 130-30 fund
c. 100-year flood
d. Free port

Chapter 16. The Twenty-First Century

17. _____ is the number of goods/services that can be purchased with a unit of currency. For example, if you had taken one dollar to a store in the 1950s, you would have been able to buy a greater number of items than you would today, indicating that you would have had a greater _____ in the 1950s. Currency can be either a commodity money, like gold or silver, or fiat currency like US dollars.

   a. Compliance cost
   b. Human Poverty Index
   c. Genuine progress indicator
   d. Purchasing power

18. The _____ theory uses the long-term equilibrium exchange rate of two currencies to equalize their purchasing power. Developed by Gustav Cassel in 1920, it is based on the law of one price: the theory states that, in ideally efficient markets, identical goods should have only one price.

This purchasing power SEM rate equalizes the purchasing power of different currencies in their home countries for a given basket of goods.

   a. Measures of national income and output
   b. Bureau of Labor Statistics
   c. Purchasing power parity
   d. Gross national product

19. _____ is an economic theory that holds that the prosperity of a nation is dependent upon its supply of capital, and that the global volume of international trade is 'unchangeable.' Economic assets or capital, are represented by bullion (gold, silver, and trade value) held by the state, which is best increased through a positive balance of trade with other nations (exports minus imports.) _____ suggests that the ruling government should advance these goals by playing a protectionist role in the economy; by encouraging exports and discouraging imports, notably through the use of tariffs and subsidies.

_____ was the dominant school of thought throughout the early modern period (from the 16th to the 18th century.)

   a. Nominal value
   b. Mercantilism
   c. Consumer theory
   d. General equilibrium theory

20. _____ was a prominent Chinese politician. As leader of the Communist Party of China, Deng became a reformer who led China towards market economics. While Deng never held office as the head of state or the head of government, he nonetheless served as the Paramount leader of the People's Republic of China from 1978 to the early 1990s.

   a. Adolph Fischer
   b. Deng Xiaoping
   c. Adam Smith
   d. Adolf Hitler

21. _____ Abd al-Majid al-Tikriti was the President of Iraq from July 16, 1979 until April 9, 2003.

A leading member of the revolutionary Ba'ath Party, which espoused secular pan-Arabism, economic modernization, and Arab socialism, Saddam played a key role in the 1968 coup that brought the party to long-term power. As vice president under the ailing General Ahmed Hassan al-Bakr, Saddam tightly controlled conflict between the government and the armed forces--at a time when many other groups were considered capable of overthrowing the government--by creating repressive security forces.

a. Adolph Fischer
b. Adam Smith
c. Adolf Hitler
d. Saddam Hussein

22. _____, Jr. (January 29, 1843 - September 14, 1901) was the 25th President of the United States, and the last veteran of the American Civil War to be elected.

By the 1880s, McKinley was a national Republican leader; his signature issue was high tariffs on imports as a formula for prosperity, as typified by his McKinley Tariff of 1890.

a. Adam Smith
b. Adolph Fischer
c. Adolf Hitler
d. William McKinley

23. The _____ is a region that spans southwestern Asia and northeastern Africa. It has no clear boundaries, often used as a synonym to Near East, in opposition to Far East. The term '_____' was popularized around 1900 in the United Kingdom.

a. 1921 recession
b. 130-30 fund
c. 100-year flood
d. Middle East

24. _____ , also known as T.R., and to the public as Teddy, was the 26th President of the United States. A leader of the Republican Party and of the Progressive Party, he was a Governor of New York and a professional historian, naturalist, explorer, hunter, author, and soldier. He is most famous for his personality: his energy, his vast range of interests and achievements, his model of masculinity, and his 'cowboy' image.

a. Adolf Hitler
b. Adam Smith
c. Theodore D. Roosevelt
d. Adolph Fischer

25. The impact of the Mexican economic crisis on the Southern Cone and Brazil was labeled the _____ .

The crisis is also known in Spanish as el error de diciembre -- The December Mistake-- a term coined by the then ex-president Carlos Salinas de Gortari. While these critics agree that a devaluation was necessary, they argue that the way it was handled was politically incorrect .

a. 1921 recession
b. 100-year flood
c. 130-30 fund
d. Tequila effect

26. _____ is a policy or ideology of violence intended to intimidate or cause terror for the purpose of 'exerting pressure on decision making by state bodies.' The term 'terror' is largely used to indicate clandestine, low-intensity violence that targets civilians and generates public fear. Thus 'terror' is distinct from asymmetric warfare, and violates the concept of a common law of war in which civilian life is regarded. The term '-ism' is used to indicate an ideology --typically one that claims its attacks are in the domain of a 'just war' concept, though most condemn such as crimes against humanity.

a. 1921 recession
b. 130-30 fund
c. 100-year flood
d. Terrorism

27. The _____ is an international organization that oversees the global financial system by following the macroeconomic policies of its member countries, in particular those with an impact on exchange rates and the balance of payments. It is an organization formed to stabilize international exchange rates and facilitate development. It also offers financial and technical assistance to its members, making it an international lender of last resort.

a. ACCRA Cost of Living Index	b. Office of Thrift Supervision
c. International Monetary Fund	d. ACEA agreement

28. The _____ is an international financial institution that provides financial and technical assistance to developing countries for development programs (e.g. bridges, roads, schools, etc.) with the stated goal of reducing poverty.

The _____ differs from the _____ Group, in that the _____ comprises only two institutions:

- International Bank for Reconstruction and Development (IBRD)
- International Development Association (IDA)

Whereas the latter incorporates these two in addition to three more:

- International Finance Corporation (IFC)
- Multilateral Investment Guarantee Agency (MIGA)
- International Centre for Settlement of Investment Disputes (ICSID)

John Maynard Keynes (right) represented the UK at the conference, and Harry Dexter White represented the US.

The _____ is one of two major financial institutions created as a result of the Bretton Woods Conference in 1944. The International Monetary Fund, a related but separate institution, is the second.

a. Financial costs of the 2003 Iraq War	b. World Bank
c. Bank-State-Branch	d. Flow to Equity-Approach

29. _____ is money accepted for exchange of goods in an economy. The prevalence of one money over another arises, usually, when a government designates through decrees that the government shall accept only particular notes and coins in payment for taxes. Typically, money of _____ consists of stamped coins and minted paper bills.

a. Totnes pound	b. Security thread
c. Local currency	d. Currency

30. The term _____ is applied broadly to a variety of situations in which some financial institutions or assets suddenly lose a large part of their value. In the 19th and early 20th centuries, many financial crises were associated with banking panics, and many recessions coincided with these panics. Other situations that are often called financial crises include stock market crashes and the bursting of other financial bubbles, currency crises, and sovereign defaults.

a. Market failure	b. Financial crisis
c. Macroeconomics	d. Co-operative economics

31. _____, often referred to by his initials _____, was the 32nd President of the United States. He was a central figure of the 20th century during a time of worldwide economic crisis and world war. Elected to four terms in office, he served from 1933 to 1945 and is the only U.S. president to have served more than two terms.

a. Adolph Fischer	b. Adam Smith
c. Adolf Hitler	d. Franklin Delano Roosevelt

32. _____, the elder son of Indira Nehru and Feroze Gandhi, was the 9th Prime Minister of India from his mother's death on 31 October 1984 until his resignation on 2 December 1989 following a general election defeat. He became the youngest Prime Minister of India when he took office (at the age of 40.)

_____ was a professional pilot for Indian Airlines before entering politics.

a. Rajiv Gandhi
c. Adolph Fischer
b. Adam Smith
d. Adolf Hitler

ANSWER KEY

Chapter 1

1. c	2. c	3. d	4. c	5. d	6. c	7. d	8. d	9. d	10. a
11. d	12. d	13. c	14. c	15. a	16. d	17. c	18. a	19. b	20. b
21. c	22. d	23. d	24. d	25. d	26. b	27. a	28. b	29. a	30. d
31. b	32. d	33. d	34. a	35. d	36. d	37. c	38. b	39. d	40. b
41. c	42. b	43. d	44. a	45. a	46. d	47. c	48. a	49. d	50. d
51. d									

Chapter 2

1. c	2. c	3. d	4. d	5. d	6. d	7. d	8. d	9. a	10. b
11. d	12. c	13. a	14. c	15. d	16. c	17. d	18. d	19. d	20. d
21. d	22. a	23. b	24. d	25. d	26. d	27. a	28. a	29. d	30. c
31. d	32. c	33. d	34. d	35. d	36. d	37. c	38. c	39. d	40. d
41. b	42. d	43. d	44. a	45. a	46. a				

Chapter 3

1. a	2. d	3. d	4. b	5. a	6. d	7. a	8. c	9. d	10. d
11. d	12. a	13. c	14. d	15. d	16. a	17. a	18. c	19. d	20. d
21. a	22. d	23. d	24. c	25. d	26. a	27. d	28. a	29. b	30. d
31. a	32. d	33. d	34. d	35. b	36. a	37. d	38. d	39. c	40. d
41. b	42. b	43. c	44. b	45. d	46. d	47. d	48. b	49. c	50. b
51. d	52. d	53. c	54. c	55. d	56. c	57. a	58. d	59. d	

Chapter 4

1. d	2. c	3. d	4. d	5. b	6. d	7. c	8. d	9. d	10. d
11. c	12. d	13. d	14. d	15. c	16. c	17. b	18. d	19. c	20. a
21. d	22. b	23. b	24. d	25. a	26. d	27. a	28. d	29. d	30. c
31. b	32. a	33. d	34. b						

Chapter 5

1. d	2. d	3. d	4. d	5. a	6. a	7. b	8. b	9. d	10. c
11. d	12. d	13. d	14. d	15. b	16. b	17. d	18. d	19. d	20. d
21. c	22. d	23. b	24. a	25. d	26. a	27. b	28. c	29. a	30. d
31. a	32. d								

Chapter 6

1. d	2. d	3. c	4. d	5. d	6. b	7. c	8. b	9. d	10. d
11. d	12. a	13. d	14. d	15. d	16. d	17. b	18. c	19. d	20. d
21. d	22. d	23. d	24. d	25. c	26. c	27. d	28. d	29. d	30. b
31. d	32. b	33. a	34. c	35. d	36. a	37. a	38. d	39. c	40. d
41. a	42. a	43. c	44. d	45. d	46. b	47. d	48. d	49. c	50. d
51. b	52. b	53. a	54. c	55. d	56. d	57. b	58. d		

Chapter 7
1. a   2. b   3. d   4. d   5. b   6. d   7. d   8. c   9. d   10. c
11. b   12. b   13. d   14. d   15. c   16. a   17. d   18. d   19. c   20. d
21. d   22. b   23. c   24. d   25. d   26. d   27. d   28. d   29. a   30. d
31. c   32. d   33. d   34. a   35. b   36. d

Chapter 8
1. d   2. c   3. d   4. c   5. a   6. b   7. d   8. c   9. d   10. a
11. a   12. d   13. d   14. a   15. a   16. b   17. c   18. d   19. b   20. d
21. d   22. a   23. d   24. d   25. c   26. d   27. d   28. d   29. c   30. d
31. c   32. d   33. d   34. d   35. d

Chapter 9
1. a   2. d   3. a   4. d   5. d   6. d   7. b   8. c   9. d   10. c
11. b   12. a   13. b   14. d

Chapter 10
1. a   2. b   3. c   4. c   5. d   6. a   7. a   8. a   9. d   10. d
11. b   12. b   13. b   14. d   15. b   16. d   17. d   18. d   19. c   20. d
21. d   22. b   23. b   24. b

Chapter 11
1. d   2. d   3. c   4. b   5. d   6. b   7. d   8. d   9. d   10. d
11. d   12. b   13. d   14. d   15. d   16. d   17. d   18. d   19. d   20. c
21. b   22. d   23. d   24. b

Chapter 12
1. a   2. d   3. a   4. b   5. d   6. a   7. a   8. d   9. d   10. b
11. a   12. b   13. b   14. d   15. b   16. d   17. d   18. d

Chapter 13
1. d   2. d   3. b   4. c   5. a   6. d   7. d   8. b   9. a   10. d
11. d   12. c   13. c   14. d   15. d   16. a   17. b   18. d   19. d   20. d
21. d   22. c   23. d   24. d   25. c   26. d   27. a   28. c   29. c   30. a
31. c   32. b   33. b   34. d

Chapter 14
1. d   2. a   3. b   4. d   5. b   6. a   7. b   8. d   9. c   10. a
11. d   12. c   13. d   14. d   15. c   16. c   17. d   18. b   19. d   20. c
21. b

ANSWER KEY

Chapter 15

1. d	2. b	3. b	4. d	5. d	6. d	7. d	8. d	9. a	10. d
11. b	12. d	13. a	14. d	15. a	16. a	17. c	18. c	19. d	20. d
21. c	22. c	23. d	24. d	25. b	26. d	27. c	28. c	29. a	30. c
31. c	32. b	33. d	34. c	35. d	36. d	37. c	38. d	39. d	40. d
41. d	42. a	43. b	44. b	45. d	46. b	47. b	48. d	49. b	50. a
51. a									

Chapter 16

1. d	2. a	3. d	4. b	5. b	6. d	7. a	8. b	9. c	10. b
11. d	12. b	13. a	14. d	15. d	16. a	17. d	18. c	19. b	20. b
21. d	22. d	23. d	24. c	25. d	26. d	27. c	28. b	29. d	30. b
31. d	32. a